DATE DUE			

EMMA WILLARD
Pioneer Educator of American Women

By Alma Lutz

*Susan B. Anthony, Rebel, Crusader,
Humanitarian*

*Created Equal, A Biography of
Elizabeth Cady Stanton*

*Challenging Years, A Memoir of
Harriot Stanton Blatch*

*With Love, Jane, Letters from
American Women on the War Fronts*

EMMA WILLARD

Pioneer Educator of American Women

by ALMA LUTZ

GREENWOOD PRESS, PUBLISHERS
WESTPORT, CONNECTICUT

Library of Congress Cataloging in Publication Data

Lutz, Alma.
    Emma Willard : pioneer educator of American women.

    Reprint. Originally published: Boston : Beacon Press,
c1964.
    Bibliography: p.
    Includes index.
    1. Willard, Emma, 1787-1870. 2. Women educators--
United States--Biography. 3. Women--Education--United
States--History--19th century. I. Title.
LA2317.W5L82 1983   376'.92'4 [B]   83-18567
ISBN 0-313-24254-2 (lib. bdg.)

Copyright © 1964 by Alma Lutz

Reprinted with the permission of Beacon Press

Reprinted in 1983 by Greenwood Press
A division of Congressional Information Service, Inc.
88 Post Road West, Westport, Connecticut 06881

Printed in the United States of America

10 9 8 7 6 5 4 3 2 1

To the Alumnae
of the Emma Willard School

With this book the author pays tribute
to the Emma Willard School on the occasion of its
one hundred and fiftieth anniversary.

Acknowledgments

I am grateful to all those who made Emma Willard's letters and other source material available to me, to Mary M. MacLear, Librarian of the Emma Willard School, to Margaret R. Meyer, Librarian of Russell Sage College, to the Connecticut Historical Society, the Historical Society of Pennsylvania, the New York Public Library, the Library of Congress, the Boston Public Library, and the New York State Library, Albany. I am indebted to Helen and William C. Hart, and to Emma Hart Dickinson Chambers, for recollections of their great-aunt, to Hewlett Scudder and John Phelps for permission to quote from letters, and to Alice Upson Cowles. I am also indebted to Anne Wellington and Clemwell Lay, former principals of the Emma Willard School, for suggesting the publication of this short biography for the one hundred and fiftieth anniversary celebration. John Lord's *Life of Emma Willard,* published in 1873 by D. Appleton & Co., has been invaluable because of its preservation of many important letters.

Preface

When we contrast the educational and professional opportunities which are open to women today as a matter of course with those so grudgingly allowed them one hundred and fifty years ago, we begin to realize what a debt of gratitude we owe to Emma Willard.

Women then were distinctly an ignorant class, but in their case, ignorance was synonymous with charm and virtue. Public opinion held firmly to the belief that education was unnecessary for women, that anything beyond the mere rudiments and a bit of embroidering, painting, or music would unsex them, undermine their health, and so menace the welfare of the race.

Emma Willard, herself eager for learning, recognized the injustice and shortsightedness of denying education to girls, and it became her life purpose to free women from ignorance and to widen their horizons. She was the first woman to take a stand publicly for the higher education of women, the first to make definite experiments to prove that they were capable of comprehending mathematics, the sciences, philosophy, and history. When, in 1819, she talked over with members of the New York Legislature her *Plan for Improving Female Education,* she probably was the first woman lobbyist. She was one of the first women to write geography, history, and astronomy textbooks, and was probably the first to provide scholarships for girls.

This story of her life, published in observance of the one hundred and fiftieth anniversary of the founding of the Emma Willard School, honors her for her vision and courageous pioneering. It is also a reminder to alumnae of the proud heritage of their school, the direct descendant of the Middlebury and Troy Female Seminaries, which played such an important role in the cultural development of our country. May it inspire them to rededicate themselves to Emma Willard's purpose—education to develop thinkers, scholarship, and high ideals.

As in Emma Willard's time, we are again facing the challenge of whether a republic can meet the needs of the times and survive. The answer may well lie in the purposeful, inspiring education offered young women, for the services and devotion of both men and women are needed to preserve free government.

ALMA LUTZ

Highmeadow
Berlin, New York

Contents

EMMA WILLARD
Pioneer Educator of American Women

1 The Heritage of Connecticut

A girl of twelve, sitting on the floor in front of the wide fireplace in the Hart farmhouse, drew geometrical figures with charcoal on the white Connecticut-marble hearth. Deep in thought, she marked off another triangle, then paused to work out the proof of a theorem. Emma Hart had made up her mind to study geometry and she was teaching herself.

For a girl to study geometry in 1800 was unusual, if not presumptuous, for it was generally assumed that women were incapable of comprehending mathematics. In fact, the study of mathematics by women was thought by many to be contrary to the will of God. The little girl, pondering over her theorems by the fireside, would in the years to come break down to a large extent the prejudices and preconceived ideas of the world in regard to the intellectual ability of women.

Emma Hart's ancestors were pioneers and courageous thinkers, and she never tired of hearing about them. Two of them, Thomas Hooker, a minister of the Church of England, and Stephen Hart, sailed from England to Massachusetts Colony for religious freedom. Then, hearing of the fertile meadows of the Connecticut Valley, they, in 1636, led a hundred men, women, and children through the wilderness to Connecticut where they founded the towns of Hartford and Farmington. Stephen's great grandson, Samuel, later moved to the Great Swamp Settlement, where on a farm near the town of Berlin, his son, Samuel, Emma's father, grew up. When his father died, leaving the family dependent upon him for support, he gave up his plans for a college education to work the farm, and at nineteen married Rebecca Norton. Soon after that, serious trouble developed between the British Government and the Colonies, and aroused by the Stamp Act, he and other young men in the neighborhood, organized Sons of Liberty Societies with the motto, "Liberty, Prosperity, and No Stamps." After the closing of the port of Boston, the Hart farm and others in Connecticut supplied Boston with

1

wheat, rye, and corn, and Captain Hart headed a company of volunteers from Berlin, sent to defend the coast towns.

The Revolution over, Samuel Hart, back on the farm, watched
with interest the building of the new nation and represented his
town in the General Assembly. By this time his wife, Rebecca, had
died and he had married Lydia Hinsdale, a capable, well-educated
young woman, ten years his junior, who took charge of his large
household with efficiency and compassion. Her daughter Emma,
born February 23, 1787, was the sixteenth child in the Hart Family.
"If baby had been a boy, we would have named him for General
Washington," Emma's father remarked to his pastor, "but under the
circumstances she will be baptized as Emma."

The simple farmhouse where Emma Hart was born, in Lower
Lane, Berlin, looked out over meadows to the clear-cut, rugged Connecticut hills. It was a square house, three stories high, red brown—
the color of unpainted, well-weathered wood. A large center chimney warmed the rooms on cold winter days. The kitchen with its
wide fireplace, shining pewter, and long pine table was the most
used room in the house. Up the spiral stairway, on the second floor
was the large loom room, always a busy place, for there were many
children to clothe and the girls of the family did their share of the
carding, spinning, and weaving. After the men had done the shear-
ing, the women sorted the wool, setting aside the best for the father's
clothes, the next best for the other men in the family, the third part
for themselves. The rest was made into flannel and blankets, while
the remnants were used for mops.

Flax, another product of the farm, was broken and dressed by
the men and spun and woven into linen by the women. The days
were always busy. Besides the regular household tasks for the girls
and farm work for the boys, autumn brought quantities of apples
and pumpkins to be pared, strung, and dried. In the spring, the kettle of maple syrup hung over the fire, boiling for sugar, and later
wild berries were gathered and preserved. Now and then, a large
iron kettle filled with soap grease was set over a fire built in the yard,
and the girls watched it boil till the soap "came" and it "spun
aprons" from the stick their mother lifted from the kettle. On hot
summer days, they sat in the cool of the house, braiding white straw
into hats, while they discussed the fashions, or perhaps how Mrs.

Lucy Brandegee fed her silkworms on leaves from her mulberry grove; how she spun, dyed, and wove a red silk gown to give to Martha Washington.

There were corn huskings, quilting bees, and house raisings. There were large family gatherings at Thanksgiving when children and grandchildren returned to the Hart home. These family gatherings stood out as red-letter days to Emma. The rows of pumpkin pies, the puddings, the doughnuts, the turkeys roasting on the spit, the cracking of butternuts by the fireside were holiday memories.

There were days when Emma and her sisters played in the meadow among the big patches of bluets and under the blossoming apple trees. They would watch the peddlers go by, their horses loaded down with big baskets of shining tinware from Edward Pattison's shop down the lane. Everybody wanted the bright new tinware, the first made in America, and peddlers traveled far West and South and even took wagonloads of tinware to Canada, bringing back furs which were made into muffs at Edward Pattison's shop.

Sometimes at Brother Asahel's on Worthington Street they saw the big yellow stagecoach drawn by four horses dash past. The blowing of the bugle, the snap of the driver's whip, the fleeting glimpses of passengers as the coach rumbled on, were reminders of a world beyond Lower Lane.

Best of all, however, were the cold winter evenings in front of the blazing logs in the big kitchen fireplace, when Emma's father told about the reading of the Declaration of Independence, about the struggles and hardships of the Revolution and the building of the new nation, about George Washington, the impulsive, daring young Lafayette, whom she particularly admired, and John Paul Jones. Emma, sitting on his knee, wide-eyed and completely absorbed, was filled with a burning patriotism which remained with her all through her life.

Often her father or mother read aloud from Chaucer, Milton, or Shakespeare, or one of her brothers or sisters read to the family, stopping in difficult parts to ask questions. Occasionally Mr. Hart brought home a book he had borrowed from a friend or from the Worthington Library. Books were rare in those days, expensive and hard to get, and the Harts treasured every one that came into their home. All of the Library's books were read at their fireside.

These books brought new ideas into the Hart home. Questions about religious and moral principles were talked over. Politics and current events were considered. There was talk about the new President, John Adams; about Alexander Hamilton and Thomas Jefferson; about the French Revolution and Napoleon and Thomas Paine's *Age of Reason*, which stirred up the minds of men and made them wonder about the things they had always believed. Captain Hart was a thinker; he was liberal; he liked to thrash out new ideas. So Emma had exciting glimpses of the world beyond Berlin, and she developed a passionate love of reading, an ability to think for herself, and an unquenchable thirst for knowledge.

Although fireside education was such an important factor in Emma Hart's life, she was not limited to this, but early attended the district school. Connecticut was one of the first of the colonies to provide public schools for primary education. The Reverend Thomas Hooker, one of Emma's ancestors, had advocated the education of children that they might learn to read the Scriptures. The early school laws, however, specified that instruction was to be for male children only. All that was considered necessary for girls was a slight knowledge of reading, which would enable them to become familiar with the Bible and the Catechism. They learned to read at home or in dame schools, conducted by elderly women in their kitchens for a few pennies a week. Emma's father, who always maintained that the state should educate its children, was sent to the Legislature as a special delegate to ask for educational measures.

The importance of more general education began to be recognized when the Republic was established, for its stability depended upon the intelligence of the voters. Although there was still opposition to the spending of public money on "schools for shes," district schools began to be opened to girls for a few months in the summer when the boys were busy on the farms. Gradually, girls were allowed to stay on through the winter months.

Emma Hart attended one of these district schools at Worthington Center. The school building was small, dilapidated, and weather-beaten; the schoolroom, plain and bare, with a fireplace on one side. A single continuous line of desks, pine boards fastened to the wall, ran around the other three sides of the room. Benches, slabs on wooden legs, formed another continuous line in front of the desks. When writing or studying, the children faced the wall with their backs to the teacher. To recite, they stepped over the benches and faced the teacher. In the middle of the room on high backless benches, the younger children sat primly and uncomfortably, their little feet dangling or struggling to touch the floor.

Describing these schooldays, Emma Hart wrote in later years: "The school house was a place of rude structure; but be it remembered, it was fully as good as the dwelling houses. The children were not enervated by luxuries at home. They came on a cold winter morning, trooping along, with the ruddy glow of health and exercise. The boys had fed the cattle, the girls had milked the cows, and made the beds in rooms which no fireplace or stove had ever disturbed; and now the bounding pulse of life beat high and strong in their veins; and they minded little the unwarmed condition of the meeting house on Sunday, or the whistling of the wind through the crevices of the school house on week days. They had learned 'to endure hardness as good soldiers.' Even the little children had begun to learn the same lesson. If no backs were provided for their seats in school, neither were there any at home to the blocks in the ample chimney corners upon which these favored ones were privileged to sit."

Emma trudged to school on cold winter days with her older brothers and sisters. Her short woven coat, a small white woolen shawl folded over her short-cropped hair and pinned at her throat, blue and white wool stockings and mittens which her grandmother had knit, heavy leather shoes—all kept her warm. She sat on the backless benches patiently for hours with other little girls who wore long, plain, straight dresses just like hers, of dark homespun, without ruffles, and covered with a blue and white checked apron tied at the waist.

The best-educated farmers in the community taught during the winter months and often the teachers were lawyers and physicians. The clergymen took a great interest in the schools, visiting them regularly and making suggestions. Reading, writing, spelling, and some arithmetic were taught. When the school assembled, the children "made their manners," the boys bowing and the girls curtseying to the teacher. Reading from the New Testament by the pupils from the oldest class down to the "ABC" children was always the first exercise of the morning. Then, while the older scholars studied, the younger ones said their letters. They had no books, and when they recited, they stood by the teacher's desk while he pointed out with his quill the letters in Webster's *Spelling Book*. The older pupils had their spelling lesson later, and for them the blue-backed *Spelling Book* was used as a reader. Besides the alphabet, many long columns of words, Roman and Arabic numerals, days of the week, months of the year, and so forth, it contained "Lessons of Easy Words, to Teach Children to Read and to Know Their Duty," such as: "Love not the world, nor the things that are in the world; for they are sin." Its "Proverbs, Counsels, and Maxims in Words of One Syllable" read: "Haste makes waste, and waste brings want," or less cheerfully but more piously: "The time will come when we must all be laid in the dust."

Next in order was a writing lesson. The children all had copybooks, made at home from large sheets of paper folded and sewed into a brown paper cover. With a ruler and homemade plummet, they lined the pages. The plummets were made by pouring molten lead into small grooves or cracks in the kitchen floor, and then smoothing off the hardened lead and sharpening it. The children brought homemade ink to school and goose quills which the schoolmaster made into pens for them. Across the top of each page of the copybooks, the teacher wrote a sentence, usually some edifying religious or moral sentiment which the pupils painstakingly copied. In the ciphering books, which were similar to the copybooks, the pupils copied rules dictated by the teacher, and problems which they had already solved, thus making their own arithmetic textbooks.

There was a short recess in the middle of the morning, first for the girls, then for the boys. During the noon hour, when school was dismissed, the children ate the lunches which they had brought with them, and then played hard at games until the sharp rapping of the teacher's ruler brought them back into the schoolroom. The afternoon's work was similar to the morning's except that the older pupils used a reader which contained extracts from standard authors and from speeches of British statesmen.

These same subjects were pursued as long as the children were able to profit from them. Gradually, grammar and geography were introduced. The Catechism, of course, was thoroughly learned. During the summer session, when the teacher was a woman, the young children brought patchwork and knitting to school and the older girls hemmed towels and tablecloths. They were especially proud of their samplers, worked in fine stitches of colored silk. When finished, they would hang in the front room at home and be used as patterns for letters in marking household linen. The difference in the ages of the pupils, the tendency to teach by rote, and the general monotony and somber religious tone of the instruction did not make the work highly interesting or inspirational. It was during these school days that Emma's father exerted such a steadying, progressive influence over her. "He was fifty years my senior," she later recalled, "yet would he often call me when at the age of fourteen from household duties by my mother's side to enjoy with him some passage of an author which pleased him, or to read over to me some essay which he had amused himself in writing."

The opening of an academy in Worthington, less than a mile from Emma's home, when she was fifteen, made a great change in the course of her life. This was one of the first academies in Connecticut incorporated by the General Assembly, and pupils came not only from Worthington, but from Kensington, New Britain, and adjoining towns. The principal, Thomas Miner, was a graduate of Yale and a teacher of ability. Both Emma and her sister, Nancy, attended the academy for two years, 1802 and 1803, and looking back, Emma observed, "I believe that no better instruction was given to girls in any school at that time, in our country."

2 The Young Schoolmistress

When Emma Hart was seventeen years old, she was asked to teach the children's school in the village. Her recollections of that first teaching experience were very vivid. "The school house," she wrote, "was situated on the great Hartford and Haven turnpike; and was surrounded on the other three sides by a mulberry grove, towards which the windows were in summer kept open. At nine o'clock, on that first morning, I seated myself among the children to begin a profession which I little thought was to last with slight interruption for forty years. That morning was the longest of my life. I began my work by trying to discover the several capacities and degrees of advancement of the children, so as to arrange them in classes; but they having been, under my predecessor, accustomed to the greatest license, would, at their option, go to the street door to look at a passing carriage, or stepping on a bench in the rear, dash out of a window, and take a lively turn in the mulberry grove. Talking did no good. Reasoning and pathetic appeals were alike unavailing. Thus the morning slowly wore away. At noon I explained this first great perplexity of my teacher-life to my friend, Mrs. Peck, who decidedly advised sound and summary chastisement. 'I cannot,' I replied; 'I never struck a child in my life.' 'It is,' she said, 'the only way, and you must.' I left her for the afternoon school with a heavy heart, still hoping I might find some way of avoiding what I could not deliberately resolve to do.

"I found the school a scene of uproar and confusion, which I vainly endeavored to quell. Just then, Jesse Peck, my friend's little son, entered with a bundle of five nice rods. As he laid them on the table before me, my courage rose; and, in the temporary silence which ensued, I laid down a few laws, the breaking of which would be followed with immediate chastisement. For a few moments the children were silent; but they had been used to threatening, and soon a boy rose from his seat, and, as he was stepping to the door, I took one of the sticks and gave him a moderate flogging; then with

8

a grip upon his arm which made him feel that I was in earnest, put him into his seat. . . . But the children still lacked faith in my words, and if my recollection serves me, I spent most of the afternoon in alternate whippings and exhortations, the former always increasing in intensity, until at last, finding the difference between capricious anger and steadfast determination, they submitted. This was the first and last of corporal punishment in that school. The next morning, and ever after, I had docile and orderly scholars. I was careful duly to send them out for recreation, to make their studies pleasant and interesting, and to praise them when they did well, and [to] mention to their parents their good behavior. Our school was soon the admiration of the neighborhood. Some of the literati of the region heard of the marvelous progress the children made, and of classes formed . . . and instruction given in higher branches; and coming to visit us, they encouraged me in my school, and gave me valuable commendation."

During this first teaching experience, Emma began to feel the need of further study to fit herself for future work. As her brother Theodore, who had become a prosperous merchant in Petersburg, Virginia, was willing to finance her education, she attended that winter the school taught by the Misses Patten in Hartford which gave instruction in "primary and essential branches" and in needlework, both lace and embroidery.

Returning to Berlin the following summer, she taught a select school for older boys and girls in an upper room of her father's house. She was then asked to take charge of the winter school in Berlin— the very same school which she had attended under Thomas Miner. Of this school, she wrote, "I had the uncommon honor [uncommon at that time for a female] to keep the winter school. . . . Whether it was four or five shillings a week which I received on that occasion, as a reward for my labors, I have forgotten. . . . Mr. and Mrs. Botsford gave me good board, (and such kind attentions as money cannot measure) for three shillings a week; such was their public spirit in favor of the school. At the close of the term, for which I had engaged, I held a public examination, which parents with encouraging zeal attended."

At nineteen, she taught both winter and summer, but found time during the spring and autumn to attend Mrs. Royse's school in Hartford as a day scholar, making her home in the family of her cousin, Dr. Sylvester Wells, who had lately moved from Kensington to Hartford. This school, established by Mrs. Lydia Bull Royse about 1800, was a celebrated institution and was said by some to be "far ahead of the Misses Patten's." Not only did the best families of Hartford send their daughters there, but pupils came from other states. Reading, writing, arithmetic, geography, French, dancing, drawing, painting, and needlework made up the cirriculum. Mrs. Royse herself gave instructions in drawing, painting and needlework, the subjects which Emma particularly wished to pursue. Tuition for fourteen weeks was $7.62, with extras for drawing and needlework materials.

Compared with the small, quiet town of Berlin, Emma found Hartford, with its brick mansions, its many shops, and numerous churches, very impressive. Living in the home of Dr. Wells, who was keenly alive to political issues and the liberal thought of his day, gave her much to think and talk about. He was a brilliant man, extreme in his views on religion and medicine, and an ardent Anti-Federalist. His move to Hartford had been made at the instigation of political friends to help in the fight against the "Standing Order." Later, as a member of the State Constitutional Convention, a State Senator, a Fellow of the Corporation of Yale College, and a candidate for Congress, he proved his abilities. A firm friendship grew up between him and Emma. They had many stimulating discussions, and he thoroughly enjoyed her keen mind and conversational ability. Eunice, his wife, was Emma's ideal, and she always thought of her as one of the most beautiful, refined, and interesting women that she had known.

Emma found French philosophy with its appeal to reason influencing Dr. Wells's religious beliefs. Its theories also appealed to her brothers, but, while she was sympathetic to these new ideas, her own views were still in a state of flux. She had been prejudiced against orthodox religion by the intolerance toward her father when he withdrew from the Congregational Church because he could no longer accept its doctrine of salvation for the few and damnation for the many. After this, he attended the Universalist Church, which preached universal salvation. Respecting, as she did, her father's deeply religious nature, she could not stray far into skepticism.

Although in the light of today, Emma Hart's girlhood seems highly peaceful and proper, it stood out against the background of the early nineteenth century in decided contrast to the generally accepted idea of what was proper for young women. While education then was far better than it had been a generation before, and women, whose mothers and grandmothers were unable to write, wrote good letters and read some books besides the Bible, nevertheless public opinion stood firmly against broadening and enlarging the educational opportunities of women. No college in the world admitted women. There were no high schools for girls. Boarding schools, which only daughters of the well-to-do were able to attend, taught the mere rudiments and stressed the accomplishments, then thought so necessary for women, such as painting, embroidery, French, a song or two for company, playing on the harpsichord, and the making of wax or shell ornaments. For poor girls, there was no education beyond the district school. Rousseau's idea was still generally accepted: "The education of women should be always relative to the men. To please, to be useful to us, to make us love and esteem them, to educate us when young and to take care of us when grown up, to advise, to console us, to render our lives easy and agreeable; these are the duties of women at all times."

Women had been taught that it was unwomanly to hold opinions on serious subjects, that men admired weak, clinging, innocent women. A woman who discussed politics or government, who held unorthodox views on religion or presumed to enter the educational sphere of men, was ridiculed as unwomanly, as aping men, and was at once scheduled for moral shipwreck. The tragic life of Mary Wollstonecraft, who in England had so strongly advocated education for women, was held up as an example of the pernicious influence of higher learning upon the morals of women.

The books of the day, published for the edification and improvement of women, impressed them with the virtue of cultivating their inferiority, reminding them of the Biblical authority for the domination of man. As most women were distinctly orthodox in their religious beliefs, they accepted these statements without protest.

Hannah More, the English poetess, who acknowledged the superiority of men, was regarded as a model of female virtue and was freely quoted, lauded, and held up as an example for every woman to emulate.

Although Emma Hart stepped out from all of these conventional ideas and limiting theories regarding women, she did it naturally and easily, with no sense of doing anything spectacular. This was undoubtedly due to the broad-minded, harmonious atmosphere of her home, for her father and all of her family encouraged her in every effort for progress. Her normal, happy girlhood stands out in vivid contrast to that of Mary Wollstonecraft, whose bitter struggle against poverty, and whose contact with the brutality of men and their tyranny over the lives of women, left their mark on her life. Little wonder that she was the tragic victim of circumstances while Emma Hart, in a newer, freer country, was able to forge ahead, surmount obstacles, and actually work out a system of rational education for girls. Mary Wollstonecraft had to some degree prepared the thought of the world for the work of Emma Hart, though Emma, even with her open mind, was unable to see beyond Mary Wollstonecraft's immorality, or to appreciate her struggle and her sincere, though apparently futile attempt to better the condition of women. Instead, she felt only condemnation, thinking Mary Wollstonecraft had by her conduct hindered the advancement of her sex. Therefore, as Emma Hart pioneered new fields for women, she was always careful to satisfy conventional minds by her perfect conduct and zeal for virtue.

3   Middlebury Female Academy

Emma Hart's unusual teaching ability gradually became known outside of Connecticut. Soon after her twentieth birthday, while she had charge of the Berlin winter school, she was invited to teach in Westfield, Massachusetts, in Middlebury, Vermont, and in Hudson, New York. All three offers were good and presented opportunities for progress in the teaching profession. She chose Westfield because it was nearest home, and in the spring became an assistant in the well-known Westfield Academy, which had been established seven years before, in 1800. "Youths of both sexes" who could "read and write in decent manner" were admitted and the enrollment was about two hundred. The tuition was three dollars a quarter with twenty-five cents extra during the fall, winter, and spring for fuel, sweeping, and so forth. Pupils boarded in the homes of the best families. Graduates of Williams College headed the Academy and were assisted for half of the year by a "female." It was this position that Emma Hart filled when she came to Westfield in 1807. Heretofore, in her short teaching experience, she had always had full charge of her schools, and could develop them at will. Westfield cramped her abilities. She knew she deserved more salary, and could do more and better work elsewhere. Middlebury's offer, giving her a chance to take full charge of a female academy was still open, and after a few months, the trustees of Westfield Academy reluctantly released her. However, she had been so well liked in Westfield, that the next spring she was asked to return and make her own terms as to salary, but she did not leave Middlebury, for life there was too interesting.

The prosperous, influential town of Middlebury, Vermont, with its wealth, culture, and fascinating social life introduced Emma to a manner of living entirely new to her. The leading families of the town with their luxurious homes, their fine horses, their parties and balls, formed a little aristocracy very dazzling to the young schoolmistress from Berlin. "I find society in a high state of cultivation—much more than any other place I was ever in," she wrote her parents. "The beaux here are, the greater part of them, men of collegiate education. . . . Among the older ladies, there are some whose manners and conversation would dignify duchesses."

The citizens of Middlebury prided themselves on their interest in education. They had a boys' academy, and Middlebury College had been established in 1800. That same year, Horatio Seymour had invited Miss Ida Strong to open a school for young ladies, similar to Miss Pierce's celebrated school in Litchfield, Connecticut, where she had studied. Its first sessions were held in the Court House, and were so well attended that funds were raised to erect a two-story building on land given by Mr. Seymour. So great was the enthusiasm over the undertaking that young men who were not able to contribute money offered their services in various ways, such as laying boardwalks across the muddy ground in front of the building. This was one of the very first schools in the country built especially for the use of girls. Pupils came from all parts of the state and from New York. After a few years, Miss Strong was obliged to give up the school because of ill health, and it was closed until the summer of 1807, when Emma Hart was called to reopen it. Meanwhile, the boys' grammar school had occupied the lower floor, and Emma began teaching in one large room in the upper story with thirty-seven pupils. Having full charge of the school, she assumed considerable responsibility for a young woman of twenty, but she was equal to it.

Her busy days and some of her problems are described in a letter written to her parents in August 1807: "I go to school generally before nine, and stay till one; come home, snatch my dinner, go again, and stay till almost sundown; come home, and dress in a great hurry to go abroad; get home about ten, fatigued enough to go to bed, and lie till seven the next morning, with hardly time enough to mend my stockings. Sunday I attend four meetings. My situation is a very trying one in some respects. It will be difficult, perhaps impossible, to avoid making enemies. To please all is impossible— as much as it would be for a person going two different ways at the same time. To please the greatest number of people, I must attend all the meetings Sunday, go to conference one or two afternoons in a week, profess to believe, among other articles of the creed, that mankind, generally speaking, will be damned. To please another set of people, I must speak in the most contemptible manner of conferences, and ridicule many of the notions of religionists, and praise many things that are disagreeable, such as dancing, playing cards, etc. In this situation I know of no better way than to follow the dictates of my conscience. This would direct me not to ridicule what others hold to be sacred; to endeavor not to treat any in such a manner as that they may have reason to be personally my enemies; to have no idea of pretending to believe what I do not believe."

Looking back in later years to her first winter in Middlebury she wrote: "The winter of 1807-8 was one of exceeding hardship for me. Although the weather was very cold, with frequent storms and much snow, I had to walk from Dr. Tudor's, where I boarded, to the academy and when there to keep my school in a large long room, formed like an ordinary ballroom, occupying the whole upper story, while the only means of gaining warmth was from an open fire, in a small fireplace in the north end. Yet that winter I had an increased and very pleasant school. When it was so cold that we could live no longer, I called all my girls on to the floor, and arranged them two and two in a long row for a country dance; and while those who could sing would strike up some stirring tune, I with one of the girls for a partner, would lead down the dance, and soon have them all in rapid motion. After which we went to our school exercises again. The school had quite an increase in the spring from different parts of the state, and amounted to sixty. Among them and from the village was a remarkable band of maidens, ranging from about twelve to fifteen."

This introduction of dancing was one example of her natural exuberance, so stimulating to her pupils, and showed her readiness to deviate from the stiff, routine methods of teaching, then so general. Enthusiastic about her work, she inspired her pupils with the desire to learn.

In her diary, she recorded the events of those days in Middlebury, often with moralizing comments. She commented on her study of history and painting, and confessed her literary aspirations. She wrote poetry, just as her father had, because she felt the need of expressing herself in verse. While teaching interested her, there are no indications that she had any particular ambition in this line or that she was evolving any definite plans for the improvement of woman's education.

After one very successful year, she began to realize that religious differences among the townspeople were threatening to undermine the school. This caused her many unhappy moments, but it was eventually cleared up, and gained for her the staunch support of friends and the admiration of one of the leading men of Middlebury, Dr. John Willard. As soon as he heard of the school difficulty, his sense of fair play was aroused and he at once championed the young schoolmistress.

Emma, essentially a hero-worshiper, was very much attracted to Dr. Willard. It was flattering to have a man of education, wealth, and social prominence come to her defense, particularly in an age when men in general had little sympathy with an independent young schoolmistress. Dr. Willard was a physician, and a man of influence in politics, a Republican. Always Republican in sympathy because that party had opposed her father's religious persecutors, Emma discovered much common ground for conversation with Dr. Willard, and instead of being disturbed by her interest in politics and government, as many men might have been, he found her a stimulating companion and was charmed by her enthusiasm.

Those were proud, joyous days of courtship for the young schoolmistress. Young beaux appeared insignificant beside this older, more experienced man. For Dr. Willard, as well, there was happiness in his companionship with Emma, whose beauty and youth held a depth of intellect and understanding that he had never before encountered.

They were married on August 10, 1809, when Emma was twenty-two. Although Dr. Willard was twenty-eight years older than she, the difference in their ages was not markedly apparent. He was vigorous, active, and in the prime of life, and Emma, in spite of her youthful appearance, was mature mentally. He had also come to Middlebury from Connecticut. He was born in East Guilford where his father, Captain John Willard, had been a shipmaster. Still a young child when his father died, he was brought up by his mother on a small farm, but as farm work was drudgery to him, he went to sea, and during the last years of the Revolution, was taken prisoner by the British. When he finally was released, he was made quartermaster of a Connecticut regiment of volunteers. After the war, he began the study of medicine under the direction of an East Guilford physician. He married Esther Wilcox, moved to Middlebury, then almost a wilderness, and soon had a successful medical practice. After a year in Middlebury, his wife died, leaving a baby boy. Some years later he married Mindwell Meiggs, a widow, and they had three children. His second wife also died within a few years.

By that time he had become dissatisfied with the practice of medicine and turned to politics, which interested him greatly. He was appointed Marshall of the District of Vermont under Jefferson's administration and was holding this position when he met Emma Hart. He was enthusiastic about Vermont and proud of its Constitution. He exercised great influence among Vermont Republicans, and when he married Emma Hart, he not only held the position of Marshal of Vermont, but was supervisor of the direct tax imposed by the Federal Government, paymaster of pensions, chairman of the Rebublican organization of Vermont, and a director of the Vermont State Bank. He also owned several farms near Middlebury and had just built a pretentious brick house on Main Street. Everything pointed to a prosperous married life for the Willards.

Emma Willard began her married life with the enthusiasm so characteristic of her. She loved and respected John Willard and was not to be disappointed in him, for he loved her devotedly and was sympathetic to all her interests. There are no indications that she regretted giving up teaching in spite of her marked abilities in that line. Like all girls of that period, her highest ambition was for a happy married life, and possibly her personal ambitions were satisfied by her dreams of Dr. Willard's political advancement.

There was, however, one cloud over their otherwise happy married life, the attitude of Dr. Willard's children toward their young stepmother. In spite of her great desire to mother and befriend them, she met antagonism, for they were obsessed with the idea that she had married their father to advance her position. The oldest of the family, Gustavus, was the same age as his stepmother. He had studied at Middlebury College in the class of 1805, and later feeling the urge to go West, had moved to Ohio. William Tell was thirteen;

Benjamin Franklin, eleven; and Laura a few years younger. Repeated rebuffs and suspicion in return for her kindness wounded Emma deeply. Remembering the affection in the Hart family toward her mother, who was the stepmother of seven, she could not understand her stepchildren's attitude toward her. It took years of patience, tact, and kindness to overcome their prejudice even in a degree.

Dr. Willard's work kept him away from home a great deal. During these absences, Emma buried herself in his library, studying dry medical volumes so that she might be able to discuss medicine and physiology intelligently with him. Delighted with her interest and ability, he encouraged her. Many an older man would have dominated and stifled the development of his young wife's personality, but not so Dr. Willard whose sympathy and understanding brought out the very best in her. They found their days together filled with happy companionship.

Mrs. Willard's disappointment in her stepchildren was somewhat alleviated by the thought of the coming of her own child. As she busied herself with household tasks in the large, "elegant" brick house on Main Street, or sat by the window sewing, looking out across the wide valley toward the encircling hills, which brought back memories of her Connecticut home, she treasured the thought that her own child would love her and crave her affection. On the twenty-eighth day of September, 1810, she held her own baby boy in her arms, and named him John Hart Willard.

The Willard home faced Middlebury College, and daily the chapel bell and calls to recitations rang out across the campus. The bells told time for Mrs. Willard, and often she watched the boys hurrying to and from classes, envying them a little their college education. One of the boys, her husband's nephew, John Willard, lived with them for four years while he attended Middlebury College. This opened up another avenue of interest. John gave her full accounts of his class work and she read his textbooks. Geometry attracted her, as it had when she was a girl of twelve, and again she began to study it by herself. When she felt that she had mastered everything in his textbook, she asked him to give her a thorough examination, for she wanted to be absolutely sure that she understood it. He found her very proficient and, encouraged by his verdict, she next undertook the study of Paley's *Moral Philosophy* and Locke's *Essay Concerning Moral Understanding.*

This close contact with the course of study in a college opened her eyes to what women were being deprived of. Heretofore, she had been interested in knowledge simply for its own sake, for the pure joy of study, and never having been discouraged in any of her efforts for higher learning, she had not grasped the situation of the average woman. She had not realized how girls were taught mere smatterings while their brothers had every educational advantage. She had proved for herself that women were able to pursue higher studies. Now, aroused by the inequality of educational opportunity and man's assumption of superiority, she began to search for a solution to the problem.

4 Middlebury Female Seminary

After three years of prosperity, the Willards were faced with serious financial reverses. The Vermont State Bank, of which Dr. Willard was a director, was robbed, and the public, suspecting the directors of being implicated in the robbery, called upon them to make up the loss. The Supreme Court rendered a judgment against them for $28,000. The greater part of this claim was later remitted by the Legislature, and the discovery of a false key in an attic, years afterward, completely vindicated the directors. Nevertheless, the general feeling toward them for some time was one of suspicion and distrust, and as a result, Dr. Willard not only lost his good reputation, but was obliged to put heavy mortgages on all his land to make good the loss. Throughout these difficulties, his wife was loyal, calming his fears, encouraging and comforting him.

These financial misfortunes came at a time when the whole country was in a state of dissatisfaction and indecision. For years both England and France had interfered with American shipping, France confiscating American cargoes and ships, and England impressing American seamen on the grounds that they were deserters from the English navy. This finally led to the War of 1812 which was entered into halfheartedly by the North and East, especially by New England, where it was felt that all that had been gained in the past would be lost by another war. There were those also who would have preferred a war with France to one with England. All these things, Dr. and Mrs. Willard discussed by their fireside, as they waited anxiously for the latest news. They rejoiced over the victories of the Frigate *Constitution* and over Perry's capture of the British fleet on Lake Erie. They read about Henry Clay from Kentucky, the eloquent young Speaker of the House, a representative of the virile, growing West, and of other young men who had entered Congress, Calhoun of South Carolina and Daniel Webster. All three were of a new generation, vigorous, intensely American, with unbounded pride in the Republic. Then came the distressing news of the burning of

Washington. They took heart when they heard that Key had written the "Star Spangled Banner" during the attack on Baltimore. Reports of spasmodic warfare continued until the signing of the Treaty of Ghent in December 1814.

All this vitally interested Emma, as the stories of the Revolution and the formation of the Republic had interested her when a child. History was being made, and history was almost a passion with her. She continued to be an insatiable reader, but Locke, Paley, and the huge volumes in her husband's medical library did not continually claim her attention, for she had a decided taste for romance. Sir Walter Scott was her favorite author and she spent hours engrossed in *Marmion*, *The Lady of the Lake*, and the *Waverley Novels*.

Many letters passed between Emma and her father during these years. He had been happy over her successful marriage and over his new grandchild. His death in August, 1813, caused her great sorrow, for they had been very close—the thoughtful, dignified old man with his progressive views and the impulsive young woman, eager for knowledge, who had as yet barely glimpsed the fulness of her ability. She comforted herself in a poem, "To the Memory of Samuel Hart," one verse of which emphasized a quality she most respected:

> He held, it was a right which free-born man
> Possessed, to freely think, and freely speak;
> Nor deemed it good inquiry to repress,
> And with authorities to silence reason;
> Nor e'er would he, dishonest to himself,
> Permit his reason thus to be subdued.

She gave considerable thought to helping her husband meet his financial obligations. Very naturally she turned to teaching and opening a boarding school for girls in her own home. When she first suggested this to Dr. Willard, he objected, but her earnestness finally convinced him that he should put aside his pride and allow her to develop in a field for which she was exceptionally well fitted. From then on he co-operated with her in every way.

In the spring of 1814, when her son was three and a half years old, she opened the school. "My leading motive," she wrote, "was to relieve my husband from financial difficulties. I had also the further motive of keeping a better school than those about me." At first, she taught the light, superficial studies then considered suitable for girls, but gradually she introduced higher subjects. Her plan was not to allow any pupil to study more than three so-called higher subjects at a time, for example, mathematics, history, and a language. The rest of the school day was to be filled with music, drawing, penmanship, and lighter studies. Eager to disprove the popular fallacy that education undermined the health of young women, she arranged the hours of study, exercise, and sleep according to her ideas of what was best for the health of the girls. Her pupils were daughters of some of the best families of the neighborhood, all enthusiastic over their work and eager to learn. They had a happy social life at the school, just as if they were one large family. Mrs. Willard with her rare conversational ability and her interest in literature made the evening sewing circle highly interesting. She read to the girls from Wordsworth, Coleridge, and Southey; sometimes a play was read or acted by the girls; and there were discussion periods in which she gave her pupils good advice and inspired them with high ideals.

This tendency to pass on good advice was not priggishness on the part of Mrs. Willard; it was characteristic of the age. A certain zeal for virtue was considered very becoming in a woman. Letters were weighed down with good advice, and not only letters from parents to children, but friendly letters written by one girl to another. Emma Willard, a married woman and a teacher, had much to impart from her experience, and she delighted in giving friendly counsel, often passing this along to her younger sister.

Emma and her younger sister, Almira, had much in common—a love of study, a special aptitude for teaching, and a great desire to progress and improve the intellectual status of women. Almira, six years Emma's junior, looked up to her as a model of virtuous, progressive womanhood. She, too, had taught in the Berlin schools and in the towns nearby. She had visited Emma in Middlebury, and they had talked over woman's meager educational opportunities, disadvantages, and possibilities. Almira had studied at the Academy in Pittsfield conducted by her cousin, Nancy Hinsdale, and came to Middlebury again, when Emma had opened her school in her own home. She was so impressed by her sister's work that when she took charge of a female academy in Sand Hill, New York, she likewise introduced higher studies. Emma's interest and solicitude followed Almira wherever she went.

Middlebury Female Seminary proved to be a great success. The enrollment was large, seventy pupils, forty of whom were boarders. Mrs. Willard had an excellent housekeeper and a good assistant teacher. Her pupils took up the higher subjects with ease and great interest, and parents were pleased with the results. They found their daughters as refined and ladylike as ever, and intelligent as well. None of the much-prophesied dire effects of education were noticeable. All this spurred Mrs. Willard on to work for a fairer, better system of education for girls. Not only did she feel the injustice of depriving girls of a good education, but she was impressed by the shortsightedness of the men. She was convinced that married life would be happier and on a higher plane if the wife were the intellectual companion of her husband. She knew that mothers whose minds and ideals had been strengthened by education would give the world better sons. She longed to share these views, but first she must be able to furnish concrete proofs by continually improving her own school. In this, she encountered difficulties. She could not afford to employ professors to teach the higher subjects. She could not ask fathers to pay too highly for their daughters' education. She appealed to Middlebury College to allow her pupils to sit as listeners in some of the classes, but this was refused. She asked if she might attend the boys' examinations to become familiar with college methods and the standard of scholarship. This too was refused on the grounds that it would be "unbecoming" and might create an unfortunate precedent. Otherwise, the president and the professors of the college took a friendly interest in her plans. There was nothing left for her to do but to evolve her own methods, to train her own teachers, to study new subjects, and to teach them herself.

In a sketch written for a friend some twenty-six years later, she described her efforts: "My exertions meanwhile, became unremitted and intense. . . . I spent from ten to twelve hours a day in teaching, and on extraordinary occasions, as preparing for examination, fifteen; besides always having under investigation some one new subject which, as I studied, I simultaneously taught to a class of my ablest pupils. Hence every new term some new study was introduced; and in all their studies, my pupils were very thoroughly trained. . . . I was wont to consider that my first duty as a teacher required of me that I should labor to make my pupils by explanation and illustration *understand* their subject, and get them warmed into it, by making them see its beauties and its advantages. During this first part of the process, I talked much more than the pupils were required to do, keeping their attention awake by frequent questions, requiring short answers from the whole class—for it was ever my maxim, if attention fails, the teacher fails. Then in the *second* stage of my teaching, I made each scholar recite, in order that she might *remember,* paying special attention to the meaning of words, and to discern whether the subject was indeed understood without mistake. Then the *third* process was to make the pupil capable of *communicating.* And doing this in a right manner was to prepare her for examination. At this time I personally examined all my classes. . . .

"Scholars thus instructed were soon capable of teaching; and here were now forming my future teachers; and some were soon capable of aiding me in arranging the new studies, which I was constantly engaged in introducing. Here I began a series of improvements in geography—separating and first teaching what could be learned from maps—then treating the various subjects of population, extent, length of rivers, etc., by comparing country with country, river with river, and city with city—making out with the assistance of my pupils, those tables which afterwards appeared in Woodbridge and Willard's *Geographies.* Here also began improvements in educational history. *Moral Philosophy* came next, with Paley for the author . . . ; and then the *Philosophy of the Mind*—Locke the author. . . ."

She also taught mathematics, and it was in Middlebury that "the stream of lady-mathematicians took its rise." As she had no model to follow, she evolved her own examinations and conducted them fearlessly, inviting the Professors of Middlebury College as well as many prominent citizens to attend. In this way, she felt she could best bring to the notice of the public the fact that the female mind could comprehend collegiate studies. To a friend, the wife of Governor Skinner, of Vermont, she wrote in 1815: "I thank you for your favorable opinion of my exertions in my school, and I am not so modest as to say that I do not think I have in some degree deserved them. Certainly, when I compare what I have done with my ideas of perfection, I have much cause to be humbled; but, when I compare my labors with what are generally done in schools of a similar kind, I feel some cause to be satisfied with my own. I am gratified with your sentiments of female education; and I wish legislators thought as you do and I do. They can expend thousands for the education of male youths, but when was anything ever done by the public to promote that of females? And what is the reason for it? It is not because the expense is valued, nor because fathers do not love their daughters as well as their sons. It is partly from inattention to the subject, and partly from the absurd prejudice that, if women's minds were cultivated, they would forget their own sphere, and intrude themselves into that of men. . . . And whence arises this? Not from a liberal and candid investigation of the organization of the female mind in general, but because a few individuals have forcibly broken through every impediment, and rivalled the men even in their own department. These, however, do not constitute the rule, but the exception. They might as well reason that, because there is now and then a brawny woman who can lift a barrel of cider, her whole sex should be kept constantly within-doors and not allowed to exercise, lest, if they should attain the full perfection of their bodily strength, they would contest the prize upon the wrestling ground, or attempt to take the scythe and the hoe from the hands of men, and turn them into the kitchen. The truth is that, when men suffer from mortification in being rivalled by women in point of strength either of body or mind, they suffer a thousand times from their weakness. How many a man has lived straitened and depressed in his circumstances, or been absolutely ruined as to his property, because his wife had a childish partiality to this place or that, . . . or because his wife wanted to appear as her neighbors appeared, without considering whether her husband's purse might compare with her neighbor's. . . . What boots it, to a man who has so weak a thing for a wife, how many elegant pieces of embroidery she may have wrought her youth . . . ? I have taken a view of woman merely as a wife; but, taking also the view as a mother, the importance of her character rises almost infinitely. When we consider that the character of the next generation will be formed by the mothers of this, how important does it become that their reason should be strengthened to overcome their insignificant vanities and prejudices, otherwise the minds of their sons, as well as of their daughters, will be tinctured by them!"

Emma Willard was roused to action. Just as her father's conviction had led him to advocate tolerance and freedom of thought in an age of religious intolerance and bigotry, just so Emma Willard was being driven by her convictions to take her stand fearlessly in the face of bitter prejudice for the education of women. Her father had instilled in her both idealism and courage. Her mother's influence had added practicality and executive ability. With these qualities at her command, she was well equipped for the contest.

5 The Plan for Improving Female Education

When Mrs. Willard had proved to her entire satisfaction her own ability and the capacity of her pupils to master difficult, so-called masculine subjects, she began to write out a plan of education which she hoped to present to the public. Her dream was to head an institution, endorsed by prominent men, an endowed institution which would receive regular appropriations from the state, as did many men's colleges. She did not dare call her ideal institution a college, because a college for women would have been considered entirely too absurd. Hearing a clergyman pray for "our seminaries of learning," she declared, "I will call it a Female Seminary. That word . . . will not create a jealousy that we mean to intrude upon the province of the men."

When she finally discussed her plans with her husband, he encouraged her, but she confided in no one else until a year after the manuscript was completed. She feared she would be regarded "as visionary almost to insanity," if she revealed her hopes and dreams. "It was not," she recalled, "merely on the strength of my arguments that I relied. I determined to inform myself and increase my personal influence and fame as a teacher, calculating that in this way I might be sought for in other places, where influential men would carry my project before some legislature, for the sake of obtaining a good school."

She was correct in her assumptions. Soon she had offers to go elsewhere. The Governor of Vermont, Cornelius P. Van Ness proposed that she come to Burlington as principal of a female seminary which was to be opened in the college buildings. As these plans did not materialize, she turned her thoughts toward New York State, realizing that the ideal situation for a seminary would be in the Hudson River valley near the head of navigation. Through several pupils from Waterford, New York, she became acquainted with General

Van Schoonhoven, who was greatly interested in her views on education and offered to show the manuscript of her *Plan* to DeWitt Clinton, then Governor of New York.

This was the opportunity for which Mrs. Willard had been
waiting. She copied the manuscript with great care and in February,
1818, sent it to Governor Clinton with an explanatory letter. The
Plan, with its many pages, was handwritten in fine clear script as
legible as print, with not a word erased or interlined. She was proud
of her beautiful penmanship and had made a special effort to perfect
it, believing it to be an important asset in her educational work.

Governor Clinton's reply assured her of his interest in her views,
and in his next message to the Legislature he recommended legislative
action to improve women's education, and referred to her *Plan*, without mentioning her name.

Mrs. Willard's friends from Waterford arranged to present the
Plan to the Legislature, but thought it best that Dr. and Mrs. Willard
spend some time in Albany during the legislative session. This they
did, and the experience was a momentous one for Mrs. Willard, then
just thirty-two years old. By request, she read her manuscript several
times to influential members of the Legislature and once before a
large group. Although this was very unconventional for a woman,
she did not hesitate, so great was her enthusiasm for her *Plan*. She
made a most favorable impression upon Governor Clinton and many
of the legislators, for she was a woman to arouse admiration and
respect. Well-dressed, handsome, with the bearing of a queen, intelligent but womanly, she impressed them not as the much-scorned
female politician but as a noble woman inspired by a great ideal. Yet,
Mrs. Willard, discussing her views on education with legislators,
was probably the first woman lobbyist.

Governor Clinton suggested that Mrs. Willard move her school
to New York State, and several prominent citizens of Waterford
urged her to come there. Day after day, she hoped for action from
the Legislature. "I had almost determined," she recalled later, "to go
in person to the legislature, and plead at their bar with my living
voice; believing that I should throw forth my whole soul in the effort
for my sex, and then sink down and die from the exertion, and that
my death might thus effect what my life had failed to accomplish."

Finally, an act was passed granting a charter to the Waterford

Academy for Young Ladies, probably the first legislative measure recognizing woman's right to higher education. The Legislature also voted to include Waterford Academy in the list of institutions to receive a share of the "literary fund" of the State, which had hitherto been divided exclusively among schools for boys. An endowment of $5,000 for Waterford Academy was recommended, but defeated by the Legislature.

Meanwhile, in 1819, Mrs. Willard had published her *Plan* in pamphlet form at her own expense under the title, *An Address to the Public; Particularly to the Members of the Legislature of New York, Proposing a Plan for Improving Female Education,* and sent it to prominent men throughout the country with the hope of arousing general interest. President Monroe and Thomas Jefferson wrote her approvingly. A note from John Adams read: "I am deeply indebted to you for your polite and obliging letter, and much more for the elegant, sentimental, and most amiable volume that attended it. The female moiety of mankind deserve as much honor, esteem and respect as the male. . . . Whenever I hear of a great man, I always inquire who was his mother, and I believe there have been very few extraordinary men who have not been cherished and guided in their morals, and their studies in their infancy, by extraordinary mothers, from the Gracchi and their mother to this time. I rejoice that the experiment has been made under the Legislature of New-York, who have done no less honor to themselves than to you. . . ."

The Honorable Duncan Campbell, a member of the Georgia Legislature, was so interested in the *Plan* that he recommended its principles to his legislature. It was also widely circulated in Europe. George Combe, then at the height of his fame, published the entire *Plan* in his *Phrenological Journal.*

The literary aspirations which the young preceptress, Emma Hart, had recorded in her diary some ten years before, were now being gratified, not through the publication of poetry as she had dreamed, but by the publication and wide circulation of her *Plan for Improving Female Education.* It was a concise, sane document, proving that the female mind could evolve a thesis, logical and clear, worthy of a legal mind. Compared with Mary Wollstonecraft's passionate appeal for the education, social equality, and independence of women in her *Vindication of the Rights of Women,* written twenty-seven years before, Emma Willard's *Plan for Improving Female Education* reads like a lawyer's brief. It is the work of a woman who, in a scientific spirit, had tested the ability of her sex and was now presenting her case.

Her purpose, she explained, was "to convince the public that a reform, with respect to female education, is necessary; that it cannot be effected by individual exertion, but that it requires the aid of the Legislature: and further, by showing the justice, the policy, and the magnanimity of such an undertaking, to persuade that body to endow a seminary for females, as the commencement of such reformation." She assured the public that she was not advocating a college for young ladies, but a seminary which would be as different from a man's college "as female character and duties are from the male."

She drew up her *Plan* in four parts: first pointing out the defects of the current system of education, then considering the principles which should regulate education, next describing a well-planned female seminary, and lastly showing what benefits society would reap from it.

She called attention to the fact that the existing schools for girls were conducted by individuals whose object was to make money and who were unable in most instances to provide suitable living quarters, adequate libraries, or other apparatus. They taught such subjects as would attract the greatest number of pupils and naturally clung to the superficial, showy, so-called accomplishments. Since qualifications for entrance, the course of study, and the school term were not regulated as in boys' academies, girls' schools were not efficiently managed and parents interfered in the course of study, choosing what they wished their daughters to learn. Often preceptresses were not the right type to guide young girls during their impressionable years, but as they were accountable to no one, they continued their harmful influence unmolested.

She pictured the daughters of the rich being hurried through the routine of superficial boarding-school studies and then introduced into the gay world with only one object in life—amusement. While these girls were "gliding through the mazes of the midnight dance," their brothers employed the lamp "to treasure up for future use the riches of ancient wisdom, or to gather strength and expansion of mind in exploring the wonderful paths of philosophy." She maintained that such a difference in education resulted in a difference in character and explained why women were looked upon as "the pampered, wayward babies of society."

Making the taste and the pleasure of men, whether good or bad, the standard for the formation of female character, was, she pointed out, a mistake, for women as well as men are independent beings. "A system of education," she said, "which leads one class of human beings to consider the approbation of another as their highest object, teaches that the rule of their conduct should be the will of beings imperfect and erring like themselves, rather than the will of God, which is the only standard of perfection."

After these bold statements, she hastened to placate those who might be offended by her unconventional views. "I would not be understood to insinuate," she added, "that we are not, in particular situations, to yield obedience to the other sex. Submission and obedience belong to every being in the universe, except the great Master of the whole. Nor is it a degrading peculiarity to our sex to be under human authority. Whenever one class of human beings derive from another the benefit of support and protection, they must pay its equivalent—obedience. . . . Neither would I be understood to mean that our sex should not seek to make themselves agreeable to the other.

"Education," she continued, "should seek to bring its subjects to the perfection of their moral, intellectual, and physical nature, in order that they may be of the greatest possible use to themselves and others; or, to use a different expression, that they may be the means of the greatest possible happiness of which they are capable, both as to what they enjoy and what they communicate."

Because the ideal seminary to which she looked forward was too large and expensive an enterprise to be carried on by an individual, she urged state aid, and recommended that the management be put in the hands of a board of trustees. It required a large building with rooms for lodging and recitations, a well-equipped library, a laboratory, and rooms for "philosophical apparatus" and the domestic department. Maps, globes, musical instruments, she considered necessary, and some good paintings which would cultivate the artistic taste of her pupils. A large staff of teachers was essential. The course of study which she advocated, she divided under four heads: Religious and Moral, Literary, Domestic, and Ornamental. She especially emphasized religious and moral instruction, mentioning tactfully that "it would be desirable that the young ladies should spend part of their Sabbaths in hearing discourses relative to the peculiar duties of their sex." She did not describe her plans for literary instruction in detail, because "such enumeration would be tedious." She did, however, strongly recommend those studies which would lead women to understand the operations of the human mind. She felt this to be extremely important in view of the fact that mothers exerted such an influence over the impressionable minds of their children. She urged the teaching of natural philosophy, so that mothers would be able to answer intelligently their children's questions about natural phenomena. She advocated domestic instruction, believing that such a department would prevent "estrangement from domestic duties." In fact, she was the originator of courses in Domestic Science. "Housewifery," she declared, "might be greatly improved by being taught, not only in practice, but in theory. Why may it not be reduced to a system as well as other arts? There are right ways of performing its various operations; and there are reasons why those ways are right; and why may not rules be formed, their reasons collected, and the whole be digested into a system to guide the learner's practice?"

The "ornamental" studies which she recommended for a seminary were music, drawing, painting, "elegant penmanship" and "the grace of motion." She did not include needlework which, in its most ornate phases, was considered an essential part of the curriculum of a girls' school. In defense of this omission, she said that she considered the use of the needle for other purposes than "the decoration of a lady's person or the convenience or neatness of her family" a waste of time, since it was of so little value in the formation of character. Music, drawing, and painting, she advocated because of their refining influence. "The grace of motion" would be learned chiefly from dancing, which would also provide exercise and that recreation essential for the "cheerfulness and contentment of youth."

In conclusion, she pointed out the benefits which would result from the establishment of female seminaries. Most important was the great improvement that she expected to see in the common schools, because many young ladies trained in the seminaries would become teachers and release from that service men whom the country needed for other work. Women would be able to give all their time to teaching, whereas men looked upon it as a temporary occupation. She felt that well-trained women would not only make better teachers than men, but could afford to accept lower salaries. "Equal pay for equal work" was not to be thought of in those days, or if it ever was, it became unimportant in the face of the more urgent need of enlarging woman's sphere. Women today are still combating the injustice and unreasonableness of that compromise made so many years ago.

Next she advanced her most deeply felt argument—that for the sake of the Republic women must be educated. She reminded her readers of the all-too-general opinion that the Republic of America could not last, that just as other republics had failed, it, too, would speedily decline and fall. Women, she maintained, gave society its tone, and the women of America could with the proper education save their country from destruction. Higher education for women would preserve the country from enervating luxuries, follies, and vices, and would build up an intelligent womanhood which would be the bulwark of society. Women of education and character would bear nobler sons and would train them for useful citizenship. Ending on this note of patriotism, she appealed to the pride of American men, urging them to lead in promoting the education of women for the future welfare of their country.

Although a few broad-minded men with imagination and vision approved of Mrs. Willard's efforts for women's education and were ready to help her, the general opinion even among her sympathizers was the usual one, that the public was not ready for such an unprecedented step. The opposition was vocal, declaring that book learning would not help women knit stockings or make puddings, and one indignant farmer entered his protest with "They'll be educating the cows next." Others feared that masculine studies, such as mathematics, sciences, the classics, and philosophy, would rob women of their charm. Still others claimed these studies would encourage women to compete with men, upset the established order, and would so impair women's health that the race would be enfeebled and the population decreased.

In spite of the opposition or indifference of the public, there was nevertheless a strong movement among women for improved education. Women were awakening and beginning to recognize their own abilities. The first faint signs of a woman's rights movement were appearing, and throughout the country, women were attempting to establish schools for girls.

Emma Willard, however, stands out pre-eminently in this movement for the higher education of women. No other woman made such definite experiments in education, or so daringly stepped into the limelight to wage her fight for education; nor was there anything at the time which compared in influence with her *Plan for Improving Female Education.*

6   The Troy Female Seminary

So hopeful was Mrs. Willard of financial aid from the New York Legislature, that in the spring of 1819, as soon as the stagecoach and wagons could make the trip over the muddy roads, she moved her school from Middlebury to Waterford, New York, where a group of interested citizens had leased a large three-story brick building for her. Even in this she had the co-operation of her husband, who willingly left his home in Middlebury to further her educational work.

Many of her Middlebury pupils were enrolled in the Waterford Academy for Young Ladies and by fall there were twenty-two boarders. Her mother spent the winter of 1820 with her at the school, happy in the large household and enjoying her nine-year-old grandson, John.

Mrs. Willard had trained several of her Middlebury pupils to assist her in teaching. This made it possible for her to devote more of her own time to the teaching of mathematics. She was convinced that mathematics more than any other subject would develop and train the minds of women, clarify and steady their thinking, and thus equip them for greater usefulness.

Eager to make her pupils thoroughly understand geometry, she cut out paper triangles for concrete illustrations. For her solid-geometry class, she carved cones and pyramids out of potatoes and turnips. As geometry textbooks were very hard to get, the pupils were entirely dependent upon Mrs. Willard's oral teaching and these figures of turnip, potato, and paper.

After taking two or three lessons in algebra from a teacher in Waterford, and finding that he could not understand or explain many of the problems, she studied by herself, determined to master it, as she had geometry. She also studied trigonometry and conics by herself, and when she felt competent, began to teach them. The introduction of mathematics to such a degree aroused a great deal of criticism and ridicule, and when one of her pupils, Mary Cramer, was publicly examined in geometry, it caused as great a stir as did woman's entry into the fields of medicine and law, years later. In fact, many insisted that Mary Cramer's examination was pure memory work, for no woman ever had been or ever would be able to understand geometry.

Mrs. Willard also continued to improve her methods of teaching geography. There were few textbooks available and those few were highly unsatisfactory. In many of the geographies, the principal cities were located by giving their distances from London, reading for example, "Pekin, the capital of China, stands 8052 miles, south-easternly from London." There were many questions such as: "What curiosities are there in France?" Each question had its answer which was to be memorized. Geography taught in this way had little appeal, and pupils expressed their boredom by writing on the fly leaves of their textbooks:

> If there should be another flood
> Then to this book I'd fly;
> If all the earth should be submerged,
> This book would still be dry.

Mrs. Willard made the subject interesting by describing the various countries and their people, and used maps and charts, which appealed to the eye rather than to the memory. At a glance the location, relative position, and population of a country or city could be seen. Map drawing was an essential part of her course. When she found that these new methods produced better results, she began work on a geography textbook, assisted by one of her pupils, Elizabeth Sherrill.

Elizabeth Sherrill's mother had been given a position in the Middlebury Female Seminary when Elizabeth was still a child, and Mrs. Willard grew very fond of her and cared for and educated her as if she had been her own daughter. Elizabeth thrived under Mrs. Willard's training and when she was only fourteen taught a few classes and drew many of the maps for Mrs. Willard's geography.

Describing the daily routine of her school, Mrs. Willard wrote: "We rise at five or six in the morning, then assemble for devotions, and then spend nearly an hour in recitations. From half-past seven to half-past eight our domestic teacher takes charge of those who are to be instructed in matters likely to increase their domestic knowledge, taking care that they write receipts of whatever cooking they do. Though not required, all my pupils belong to this department. Our study-hours are from nine till twelve, and from two till five in the afternoon, and from eight till nine in the evening. The young ladies who board with me study in their rooms; but they are not permitted to have loud talking, or any disorder, or to pass from room to room in school-hours. As our house is large, we are enabled to have different recitation-rooms for the different classes. One of our teachers is wholly devoted to the ornamental branches. Our terms are forty-two dollars per quarter for board and tuition in all the branches taught, except music and dancing. Music is ten dollars extra per quarter. The pupils furnish their own bed and bedding; we wish them also to furnish their own spoons, knives and forks, and candle-sticks."

While Mrs. Willard's thoughts were first and foremost on the building up of her school and the working out of her *Plan for Improving Female Education,* she also kept up her interest in history and world affairs. Her study of the Bible led her to reflect upon the prophecies which heralded universal peace and the gathering of the nations in Jerusalem. She wrote out her ideas on this subject, and in 1820, published them under the title, *Universal Peace to be Introduced by a Confederacy of Nations, Meeting at Jerusalem.* Forty years later, she developed this thesis more fully and seriously, but she did not dare advance this first effort except as a work of imagination.

After Waterford Academy had been in session for about a year, Governor Clinton again appealed to the Legislature for an appropriation to enable it to continue its good work, and although a bill granting the school $2,000 was passed by the Senate, it failed in the Assembly, and the Regents of the University decided that no part of the "literary fund" should go to the Academy. Not only was this a bitter disappointment to Mrs. Willard, but it was alarming as well, for so confident had she been of financial assistance from the State that she had let the expenses of the school exceed its income.

She had always idealized her country's lawmakers, but now disillusioned, she wrote: "Once I was proud of speaking of the Legisla-

ture as the 'Fathers of the State. . . .' I knew nothing of the ma-
neuvers of politicians. This winter has served to disenchant me. My
present impression is, that my cause is better rested with the people
than with their rulers. I do not regret bringing it before the Legislature, because in no other way could it have come so fairly before the
public. But when the people shall become convinced of the justice
and expediency of placing both sexes more nearly on an equality,
with respect to privilege of education, then Legislators will find it
their interest to make the proper provision."

In 1821, the Trustees of Waterford Academy again unsuccessfully petitioned the Legislature for funds. Then Mrs. Willard began
to listen to offers from influential citizens of Troy, New York, who
were urging her to move her school there and were promising her
financial assistance. The lease of the Academy building was to expire
in May. Neither the citizens of Waterford nor the Legislature had
provided the funds necessary for its renewal and Dr. and Mrs.
Willard were unable to meet this expense alone. The overtures from
Troy were a godsend. "It seems now," she wrote her mother, "as if
Providence had opened the way for the permanent establishment of
the school on the plan which I wish to execute. I believe, if Troy
will give the building, the Legislature will grant the endowment."

Troy, in 1821, with a population of about five thousand, was a
thriving, prosperous city, one of the most enterprising cities outside
of New England. Because of its cotton mills, its nail factory, paper
mill, soap factory, its tanneries and potteries, it was looked upon as
one of the manufacturing centers of the country. Its situation as an
inland port on the upper Hudson River was a tremendous asset com-
mercially in the days before the coming of the railroad. The Erie
Canal, then in the process of construction, promised further opportunities for commercial development, since it would connect Troy
with the vast unsettled territory to the West. The citizens of Troy
were awake to the possibilities of building up their city and realized
the importance of encouraging education and the arts as well as business. A school, such as Mrs. Willard proposed, appealed to their progressive spirit. There was no school like it in the country. While few
of Troy's citizens were moved by any great sympathy for the educa-

tion of women or for Mrs. Willard's plans for the improvement of her sex, they were able to appreciate her business and executive ability. They made her generous offers and she accepted them.

On March 26, 1821, the Common Council of Troy passed a resolution to raise $4,000 by special tax for the purchase or erection of a suitable building for a female seminary.

Moulton's Coffee House on Second Street opposite the Court House was purchased in April. It was a three-story wooden building with twenty-two rooms and a large ballroom, centrally located and near the churches and public buildings. Additional money needed for the purchase and for repairs was raised by subscription. The Common Council of Troy then appointed a Board of Trustees and they in turn appointed a Committee of Ladies who were occasionally to confer with Mrs. Willard regarding the school. This progressive step aroused a real interest in education among the women of Troy.

The work of remodeling began at once. The old building was stripped of its weatherboarding and bricked, and the interior was rearranged according to Mrs. Willard's suggestions. "I want you to make me a building which will suit my trade," she told the Trustees, "and then I will not complain provided you finish it so that we do not get slivers into our fingers, from rough boards. I expect the life of the school will be on the inside, and not on the out; and when the school wants to grow, you must enlarge its shell." Although the school was Mrs. Willard's, the legal status of married women, at that time, made it necessary to lease all of the property to Dr. Willard. The rent was $400 a year, and this was to be used by the Trustees for paying interest on loans and for making repairs.

Mrs. Willard moved her school to Troy before the building was finished, finding temporary living quarters in two houses nearby, and teaching in the lecture room of the Troy Lyceum of Natural History. In September the Troy Female Seminary was officially opened in permanent quarters, enrolling ninety young ladies representing the leading families of New York State, Massachusetts, Vermont, Connecticut, Ohio, South Carolina, and Georgia. Twenty-nine were residents of Troy.

Mrs. Willard was thirty-four years old at this time. She was a woman to inspire confidence: charming in manner, handsome, and vigorous. Not only did she make a most favorable impression upon parents, but her pupils idealized her and were fired with ambition by her enthusiasm.

As the need for financial assistance continued, she again appealed to the New York Legislature for an appropriation and again was ignored. However, the citizens of Troy came to the rescue. Their interest and the increasing popularity of the Seminary made it possible for her to succeed without State aid. Her domestic life also was increasingly happy. Dr. Willard, never jealous of her success, aided her in every possible way and made himself indispensable as business manager and school physician.

She was now assisted by a professor who taught the modern languages, painting, and music, and by a number of teachers, most of whom she had trained herself. To have employed educated men as professors would have been a prohibitive expense, and besides, she felt that teachers educated by her were better adapted to reach the untrained minds of young girls. She took definite steps to improve the curriculum, adding advanced courses in history and natural philosophy. No school for girls in the country offered such a complete course of study. She continued her system of studying and teaching mathematics, staying a few lessons ahead of the classes she taught. Proud of the ability of her pupils, she often told how one or two of them, who had more time for study than she, got ahead of her occasionally in the solution of an algebra problem. Her methods of teaching geography were decidedly original, and she tested her theories as she taught. Well satisfied with her results, she resumed her interrupted work on the geography textbook which she had begun in Waterford, New York.

Meanwhile, William Channing Woodbridge, who was also preparing a geography, heard of her undertaking. Their theories and methods of teaching proved to be so similar that they decided to collaborate, and in 1822 published *A System of Universal Geography on the Principles of Comparison and Classification.* Mrs. Willard's contribution to the book was the section on Ancient Geography "accompanied with an atlas," also problems on the globes, and rules for the construction of maps. In the Preface, Mrs. Willard pointed out the advantages of her new method of teaching geography with maps and charts, maintaining that by appealing to the eye rather than to memory facts were acquired with greater ease and were retained longer. "It is nearly eight years," she said, "since I began to teach geography by this method. Intending to publish my plan of instruction, I carefully watched its operation in the minds of my pupils, . . . and my success in teaching it far surpassed my expectation."

Woodbridge and Willard's *Geography* attracted a great deal of favorable attention and was widely circulated, as it met a great need in the schools. It was by far the best geography available at the time, making the subject much more interesting to pupils, though its presentation of facts in the stilted style of the period and its lack of pictures would repel a twentieth-century boy or girl. The success of this book not only brought Mrs. Willard a substantial financial return but also increased her prestige as an educator, as did an article of hers entitled, "Will Scientific Education Make Woman Lose Her Dependence on Man?" published in the *Literary Magazine* of New York.

To supervise the lives as well as the studies of the large number of young ladies attending the Troy Female Seminary was a colossal undertaking, but here Mrs. Willard's executive ability served her well. It was one of her theories that girls lived more naturally and normally two by two in small rooms than in large dormitories, and she had the building arranged accordingly. The two upper stories were divided into forty lodging and study rooms for the girls and teachers. The uncarpeted rooms were comfortably though simply furnished, each with a low-post double bed, a painted bureau, two chairs, and a box stove for wood. The girls were to regard their rooms as their homes and keep them in perfect order. They lit their fires from a pan of coals in the hall and filled their water pitchers from the pump in the yard. Each roommate was responsible for the room for a week at a time, and if the student monitor in her hourly round found anything out of place, a fault mark was recorded against the careless girl. The inspection of rooms was rigid. No gloves were to be found on the bureau, nor books on the bed. No girl in a thoughtless moment could sit on her bed or leave a towel on a chair without a demerit. The student monitors were part of Mrs. Willard's experiment in self-government which she felt would prepare students for life. They reported their findings to a teacher, serving as Officer of the Week, who in turn reported to Mrs. Willard at the Friday evening teachers' meeting. This plan worked very well in spite of prophecies that the girls would band together and deceive the teachers.

On the first floor of the school building were the dining room, which also served as a dancing hall, the kitchen, the laundry, and a room where the pupils were taught pastry cooking, a lecture room and a few small rooms for musical instruments. The chapel was on the second floor as were the large examination room and the rooms occupied by the Willard family.

Tuition varied according to the studies pursued. Board, including bed and bedding, furniture for room, and light, was furnished at $2.50 a week, but the catalogue also specified, "If any should prefer paying a stipulated sum by the year, they can be furnished with board including bed and bedding, furniture for the room, fuel, light, room rent, washing, and tuition in the first and second class of English studies at $200. . . . Boarders are to furnish themselves with a tablespoon, a teaspoon, and towels."

Life at the Troy Female Seminary was strictly regulated. The rising bell sounded at six-thirty every morning in the summer; in the winter, at seven. The girls then assembled for half an hour of study, and half an hour of exercise in the dormitory or park. Breakfast was at eight. Study hours and recitations followed until twelve when a substantial dinner was served. At four, school was dismissed with a prayer offered by Mrs. Willard, and then the girls had two free hours which they spent walking, visiting, or attending to their wardrobes. After their six-o'clock supper and before commencing their evening studies, they danced for an hour, their curls bobbing and their swiftly moving slippered feet peeping modestly from beneath the long full skirts of their plain, high-waisted muslin dresses. Mrs. Willard, looking on, would beam with satisfaction at the graceful movements of her rosy-cheeked girls, more firmly convinced than ever that dancing was a most useful exercise and relaxation. At a time when weak, delicate, fainting women were the fashion, her girls were vigorous, proving that education did not undermine their health.

Simplicity of dress was another of Mrs. Willard's rules. The school catalogue read: "Mrs. Willard wishes the dress of her pupils during school hours to consist of calico, gingham, or crape, made in plain style. Parents and guardians are earnestly requested not to furnish their daughters or wards with expensive laces, jewelry, or any other needless articles of apparel, nor to leave with them the control of money." Any girl who attempted to overdress received a demerit. Mrs. Willard had no patience with so-called fashionable schools that encouraged luxury and interest in furbelows. Her girls were to be sensible and intelligent, a credit to their sex. This did not mean that they were to pay no attention to their looks. She laid particular stress on good manners and personal appearance, for it was her firm belief that it was every woman's duty to be as beautiful as possible, not to satisfy her vanity or to please man, but "to glorify her Maker," to be a pleasure to her friends, and to increase her influence. In well-planned lectures, she impressed her pupils with their social duties and tried to develop qualities which would make them attractive, interesting, and influential. She taught them how to enter and leave a room properly, how to rise and be seated gracefully. She watched their table manners. She was very patient with awkward girls and gave them private instructions. She herself practiced what she preached, and was always well dressed, in plain black, with a white surplice.

Religious instruction in the school was nonsectarian, but church attendance was compulsory. Parents selected the church which their daughters were to attend. Mrs. Willard, having outgrown the doubts and skepticism of her youth, had become a member of the Episcopal Church. Although deeply religious, she was very careful not to force her own particular church upon her pupils and was firmly resolved that the school should always remain nonsectarian. Every morning or evening, the girls read a chapter in the Bible, and Sunday mornings, as they filed into prayers, each girl handed Mrs. Willard a slip of paper on which she had written a Bible verse selected from her reading. In speaking to them about reading the Bible, Mrs. Willard said, "You must read it as a special letter from God to yourself." Her praise of the twelfth chapter of Romans led them to memorize it in full. Sunday afternoons, they gathered for further religious instructions and recited lessons from the Bible or from Paley's *Evidences of Christianity*. Young ladies of 1823 were distinctly religious. The somber tone of Paley did not depress them.

Every Saturday they assembled to hear Mrs. Willard's weekly lecture in which she impressed upon them not only their religious duties but also the "peculiar duties" of their sex. This lecture she considered more important than any other, for as she expressed it, "It is here the opinions of our little public are more formed and guided than anywhere else."

7 Emma Willard's "Daughters"

Mrs. Willard loved her girls and thought of them as her "daughters." She was vitally interested in their development and their plans for the future. The girls of 1823, like the girls of today, played pranks, looked forward to Wednesday's fresh gingerbread and Friday's applesauce, had their fads and fashions, smuggled in forbidden delicacies, and feigned terror over the Friday evening teachers' meetings, which they called the "Inquisition," and Mrs. Willard understood this side of their lives. Her courtly bearing and her dignity might at first seem to hold her aloof from them, but she felt near them, and always won their confidence and affection. The girls looked up to her as if she were a queen or a goddess, and imitated her studied, finished manners. Any girl who received special attention from her was looked upon with envy, and one who was chosen to walk to church with her was sublimely happy and proud.

Many of her girls were far from home, some from the South, some "Western girls" from the interior of New York State and Ohio, who made the long journey by stage and canalboat. In those days, when travel was so difficult, it seemed best for them to spend their vacations at the Seminary, and often they lived there several years before returning home. They needed a principal who would mother them and this Mrs. Willard did instinctively. One day a very young girl who had just lost her mother came to the Seminary. Forlorn and heartbroken, she struggled to adjust herself to her new life. Mrs. Willard, sensing her grief and homesickness, took the girl into her own living quarters, and watched over her until the sharp edge of her sorrow had worn off. There were countless such examples of her human interest and kindness.

When the girls needed reprimanding, Mrs. Willard sent for them singly, and instead of condemning them, she talked quietly with them emphasizing their good qualities and arousing in them a determination to do better. "Do your best and your best will be growing better," was one of her favorite maxims. To a pupil who com-

plained that unkind things were being said about her, she quoted
these lines from Pope:

> "Trust not yourself, but your defects to know,
> Make use of every friend and every foe."

Her interest in her "daughters" continued after they left the Seminary, and she corresponded with many of them.

Her "daughters" were of various types—rich and poor, frivolous
and serious, young and old, some destined for society, others eager to
become teachers. The Troy Female Seminary attracted not only
daughters of wealthy and prominent families, but girls from frontier
settlements, and poor girls who had struggled and economized to attend at least one term. The average age of the students was seventeen, but there were also many older girls, some teachers, some young
widows who wished to add to their meager education. Daughters of
Troy clergymen were given free instruction and daughters of other
clergymen received a large reduction in tuition, as did many girls
who were studying to become teachers.

Mrs. Willard could well be proud of the prominent names
among her pupils. Daughters of Governors Van Ness and Skinner
of Vermont, Governor Cass of Michigan, and Governor Worthington
of Ohio were enrolled. Effie, Catherine, and Sarah Irving, nieces of
Washington Irving, spent several years at the Seminary. Aaron Burr
brought his nieces to visit, and Mary Wollstonecraft, niece and name-
sake of the famous Mary Wollstonecraft, spent a few years at the
Seminary after a very tragic girlhood. Her father, Captain Wollstonecraft, had come to this country in 1812, had settled and then
married at West Point. He took his five-year-old daughter with him
on a journey to New Orleans, contracted yellow fever, and died, leaving her helpless among strangers. She was bound to a Baptist minister and his wife, who treated her cruelly and would not allow her to
learn to read. Finally through an advertisement in a New Orleans
paper, offering a large reward, her mother recovered her, took her
back to West Point, and later sent her to the Troy Female Seminary.

Many of Mrs. Willard's nieces were given a home in the
Seminary. Mary Lydia Treat, the daughter of her sister, Lydia,

came to the Seminary when she was twelve years old, and Mrs. Willard adopted her as she later adopted Emma Willard Hart, the motherless daughter of her half brother, Jesse. Both eventually became teachers at the Seminary.

She received many applications from girls who could not afford to pay their tuition, but who longed to study and become teachers. Many of them were accepted at the Seminary and given free instruction. Some were even provided with suitable clothing, and sometimes with traveling expenses. The girls in turn contracted to repay their tuition gradually when they became teachers, as this would enable other girls to have similar opportunities for study. Rich and poor were treated alike and no one ever knew which girls received free tuition. It was one of Mrs. Willard's greatest joys to help girls who longed for an education, and because her judgment was very keen, she seldom chose an applicant who proved disappointing. A girl who sent her a careless, poorly written letter was at once rejected. Through the years she loaned approximately $75,000 to young women for their education and was probably the first woman to provide scholarships.

She was also one of the first educators in the country who took definite steps to train teachers. Because she knew that there was a crying need for efficient teachers in the rapidly expanding West, she felt it her duty to provide as many as possible. She encouraged young women to become teachers who otherwise would have spent their days in idleness or the social round, and urged those in moderate circumstances, who would always be dependent upon a male relative, to support themselves by teaching and thus not only benefit society but improve their own status.

As early as 1814, when she opened the Seminary in Middlebury, she had begun to train pupils to assist her in teaching, and this phase of her work gradually developed to such an extent in the Troy Female Seminary that she furnished teachers for schools in all parts of the country. A school certificate signed "Emma Willard" was considered the highest recommendation a teacher could have. The Troy Female Seminary may well be called the forerunner of the normal school, and teachers' college. In fact, Mrs. Willard considered it the first normal school. She said: "I continued to educate and send forth teachers, until two hundred had gone from the Troy Seminary before one was educated in any public normal school in the United States. Thus early was my system of female education carried to every part of the country, and the school which, in 1814, was begun in Middlebury is fairly entitled to the honor of being the first normal school in the United States."

Sending her Seminary pupils out into the world to teach moved her deeply, inspiring this poem:

> To a Young Lady
> About to Leave me, to Take Charge of a Female Academy.
>
> And thou dost leave me, Julia, and thy course
> Wend far away? Go, in the name of God.
> Prosper, and prove a pillar in the cause
> Of woman. Lend thy aid to waken her
> From the long trance of ages. Make her feel
> She too hath God's own image, and the fount
> Of the mind's grand and beautiful, is hers.
> She, too, should learn her Maker's works and will;
> Her first, best homage and obedience, His.

Although she was primarily concerned in training and developing the minds of her girls, she also wanted them to be skillful and happy in the so-called womanly tasks. Maids did not tidy the girls' rooms nor make their beds. The girls did this themselves and it was considered an important part of the day's work. Rich Southern girls, who had never before touched a broom or a duster, took great pride in cleaning their rooms. There was no hurried bedmaking at the Troy Female Seminary. Every bed must be smooth and trim. The girls often told how Mrs. Willard taught them to make a bed, advising the use of a broom handle to smooth it toward the top, in case ordinary methods failed to make it smooth enough. Their womanly interest in handwork was also encouraged. They created marvelous workboxes covered with floral decorations and painted "mourning pictures" in memory of departed relatives and friends. These pictures painted in water colors on China silk, not only portrayed the likeness of the departed, but often depicted the death scene itself. Such uncheerful occupation did not seem to fill the girls with gloom. Their religious training often centered their thoughts on death and they seemed to enjoy the contemplation of it, or perhaps it was a comfort to them to relieve their feelings in funereal poetry and "mourning pictures." Although Mrs. Willard heartily disapproved of the hours spent in fashionable schools on useless painting, embroidery, and the making of shell ornaments, she evidently believed that the usefulness of workboxes and the solemnity of mourning pictures justified them. She was willing to yield in a degree to the popular demand for such accomplishments and considered the time spent on them relaxation after the higher studies.

Even in those days girls were interested in presidential elections, although they were not supposed to be. During the campaign of Adams and Jackson, when the feelings of the nation were at a high pitch, some of the Seminary girls held a secret meeting, made dramatic speeches, and stirred up considerable political animosity. Some were staunch supporters of the safe, refined, scholarly John Quincy Adams. Others were swept away with enthusiasm for their picturesque Western hero from Tennessee, Andrew Jackson, who was the friend of the plain people. When Mrs. Willard heard of this indiscretion, she reminded the girls of the duties of their sex and pointed out to them what she considered the differences in the duties of men and women. She was not going to have her girls called "hyenas in petticoats," nor was her school to encourage that much-scorned movement for woman's rights. She could not let such things creep in to endanger the cause of woman's education. She agreed with the sentiments of *The Female Friend,* a little book widely recommended for young ladies, that "a female politician is only less disgusting than a female infidel." She tried to help her pupils understand this by comparing man to the oak and woman to the apple tree, and by explaining that the oak could never be the apple tree nor the apple tree the oak, but each could be beautiful and useful as a tree.

Thus, a woman with remarkable vision and zeal for the advancement of her sex, closed the door of her mind for a time to the consideration of women's political rights. Convinced that education must come first and that nothing should be done to cast the higher education of women into disrepute, she used great caution in allying herself with other reform movements. In fact, to her nothing seemed as important as women's education. She read the signs of the times accurately. Tradition and prejudice would yield slowly, and her efforts encountered opposition from women as well as men. She knew that women must be prepared for the freedom which was bound to come to them in this new country, the Republic of America, as she loved to call it. She would prepare them for their new freedom. Therefore Emma Willard's "daughters" were taught to be apple trees, not oaks; to improve their minds; to be beautiful, influential, and useful; to follow the example of Hannah More and Mrs. Hemans; and to stay virtuously in the distinct and separate sphere which, it was then thought, their Maker had ordained for them.

8 The Widening Influence of the Troy Female Seminary

While "female politicians" were scorned at the Troy Female Seminary, "female patriots" were nurtured there. So ardent a patriot and hero-worshiper as Emma Willard naturally instilled these same qualities in her pupils. When in the fall of 1824, Lafayette began his triumphal tour of the United States, Mrs. Willard's enthusiasm for him was revived. All her life, she had idealized Lafayette. As a child on her father's knee, she had listened spellbound to stories of the Revolution, of young Lafayette's dramatic and gallant part in it, of his friendship with Washington. She had heard stories of the French soldiers on their march through Connecticut; of their camps at Hartford, Farmington, and Southington; of the gratitude and enthusiasm of the Americans as they greeted their allies. All the childhood glamor remained. Later, her interest in history and current events had led her to follow Lafayette's career in France—his share in the French Revolution, his efforts for constitutional liberty, his sufferings in an Austrian prison. Now, this same Lafayette, this apostle of liberty, this savior of America, was coming to Troy. Mrs. Willard invited him to visit the Seminary; she wanted to show him that unique American institution. The girls were prepared for his visit. In their history classes, they were told how he came to America, as a boy of nineteen, to champion the cause of liberty.

At last, the day came when Lafayette was to honor Troy. The girls, dressed in white with blue sashes, each wearing a satin badge upon which the face of Lafayette was painted, breathlessly awaited his arrival. Across the park in front of the Seminary, an arbor, covered with evergreens and flowers, had been constructed by the ladies of Troy. Over its entrance were the words: "America

commands her Daughters to welcome their Deliverer, Lafayette."
Over the Seminary doorway, similarly decorated, a banner read: "We
owe our schools to Freedom; Freedom to Lafayette."

The guns boomed at noon, announcing the arrival of the General on the canalboat, *Schenectady Packet*. Loud continuous cheering and the rousing strains of military bands told of his triumphal ride through the streets to the Troy House where he was to be received by the Common Council of Troy and the Royal Arch Masons. While he was at luncheon, he received this message: "The Ladies of Troy, having assembled at the Female Seminary, have selected from this their number a committee to request General Lafayette that he would grant them an opportunity of beholding in his person, their own, and their country's generous and beloved benefactor."

He was escorted by Colonel Lane to the arbor in front of the Seminary where a committee of ladies, headed by Mrs. Albert Pawling, welcomed him. After expressing his joy at being so cordially received by the ladies of Troy, General Lafayette was escorted to the steps of the Seminary where he was presented to Mrs. Willard by Mrs. Pawling. In front of him in the hallway stood the pupils of the Seminary, who greeted him with a song of welcome, written by Mrs. Willard:

> And art thou, then, dear Hero come?
> And do our eyes behold the man,
>   Who nerved his arm and bared his breast
> For us, ere yet our life began?
>   For us and for our native land,
> Thy youthful valor dared the war;
>   And now, in winter of thine age,
> Thou'st come and left thy lov'd ones far.

CHORUS:

> Then deep and dear thy welcome be;
> Nor think thy daughters far from thee:
>   Columbia's daughters, lo! we bend,
>   And claim to call thee Father, Friend!

> But was't our country's rights alone
> Impell'd Fayette to Freedom's van!
>   No! 'twas the love of human kind—
> It was the sacred cause of man—

It was the benevolence sublime,
Like that which sways the Eternal mind!
And benefactor of the world,
He shed his blood for all mankind!

CHORUS:

Then deep and dear thy welcome be;
Nor think thy daughters far from thee:
Daughters of human kind we bend,
And claim to call thee Father, Friend!

At the close of the song, two of the girls—the daughters of Governor Cass of Michigan and of Governor Van Ness of Vermont—stepped forward and presented him with a copy of Mrs. Willard's *Plan for Improving Female Education* and with a copy of the verses just sung, beautifully printed on a sheet of embossed paper, bordered with blue.

Deeply moved and with tears in his eyes, General Lafayette said to Mrs. Willard, "I cannot express what I feel on this occasion; but will you, Madam, present me with three copies of those lines, to be given by me, as from you, to my three daughters?" Then he shook hands with the pupils, saying a few friendly words to each one. When it was time for him to leave, Mrs. Willard and the Committee of Ladies led him through the arbor to the street, the pupils following, "harmoniously raising to heaven their grateful voices," as a contemporary reported.

On July 1, 1825, Lafayette again passed through Troy and called at the Troy Female Seminary. According to the Troy *Sentinel,* he was received "with great propriety by the respectable lady principal" and "after gratifying the amiable members of the school with another sight of the friend of their country, he returned to the Troy House, where a delegation from Albany met him and took him into their carriage as he bid farewell to Troy."

Lafayette's visits not only brought great personal joy to Mrs. Willard, but gave the Seminary a certain fame and prestige which widened its sphere of influence. Lafayette, always interested in everything which tended to improve society, was greatly impressed by this unique venture in female education and spoke enthusiastically about it in France. So touched was he by his welcome at the Seminary, that he sent Mrs. Willard a most cordial invitation to visit his family, and thereafter carried on a friendly correspondence with her.

A letter from Lafayette was always a great event at the Seminary. Mrs. Willard called her pupils together, and enthroned before them, regal in black silk, read it aloud with great dignity and feeling. Then, they in turn reverently transcribed it. In reply to her suggestion that he send his daughters to the Troy Female Seminary, Lafayette wrote, October 29, 1827: "Your kind letter, July 31st, has afforded me the double gratification I shall ever find in the testimonies of your friendship and of your confidence. . . .

"My three daughters have been highly sensible of your goodness in the affectionate wish you have been pleased to express. Should it be possible to part with the young women, there is no person on either side of the Atlantic from whom such a proposal would be more welcome and highly appreciated. I wish, dear madam, we could receive you under our friendly roof of La Grange, where my daughters love to recall the happy memories of Troy, and singing what has been my delight to hear from my amiable young friends, to whom I beg you to offer my best regards and good wishes. My son begs to be respectfully remembered to you, in which sentiments the whole American colony of La Grange join most cordially."

This letter was signed, "Your affectionate and grateful friend, Lafayette."

Another man of influence who was of great help to Mrs. Willard at this time was Professor Amos B. Eaton, whose popular lectures and field work in botany, geology, and mineralogy had aroused great interest in the natural sciences. He had been called from Williams College in 1818 by Governor Clinton of New York to give a course of scientific lectures before the Legislature in Albany. His subsequent lectures in Troy led to the establishment of the Lyceum of Natural History, where Mrs. Willard held classes before her school building was ready for occupancy. Professor Eaton felt extremely friendly toward the education of women and was the first man to accept women as students of science. Mrs. Willard naturally turned to him to increase her knowledge of the sciences. He was amazed at her capacity for study, her earnestness, her mental keenness, her memory, and her ability to turn from one subject to another. Their methods of teaching were similar. Both strove to get away from pure memory work, to encourage reasoning and experimentation, and to make education applicable to life. Their evenings of study together must have been highly profitable to both: Professor Eaton eagerly watching the aptitude and progress of a brilliant woman, Mrs. Willard stimulated by the vigorous personality of an enthusiastic scientist. Their exchange of opinions, scholar to scholar, not as man to woman, inferior mentally, meant a great deal to Mrs. Willard. She called him "the republican philosopher," because of his simple tastes and habits and his vast fund of knowledge.

At Professor Eaton's suggestion, she introduced into the curriculum of the Troy Female Seminary courses in science which were in advance of those in most men's colleges. He took charge of this new department and taught at the Seminary until women had been trained to teach the sciences. In 1822, he published a *Zoological Syllabus* especially for the Troy Female Seminary, and dedicated his *Chemical Instructor* to Mrs. Willard and Dr. Beck. When, early in 1825, Stephen Van Rensselaer, who had been greatly impressed by Professor Eaton's work and ability, established the Rensselaer School, later the Rensselaer Polytechnic Institute, and made Professor Eaton its Senior Professor, Mrs. Willard's opportunities for study with him increased, and Seminary students attended some of his lectures.

It was about this time that Mary Lyon, whose interest in science had been aroused by Professor Eaton's lectures at Amherst, spent a summer in Troy with his family, continuing her studies. She met Mrs. Willard, but unfortunately no records have so far been found of the impression these two pioneer educators made upon each other.

Mrs. Willard's sister, Almira, also studied with Amos Eaton. In fact, she became one of his outstanding pupils, contributing more to science than any other woman of that period in America. Her progress was rapid, and she was soon teaching botany at the Seminary, and later, chemistry and geology. She had married Simeon Lincoln, editor of the *Connecticut Mirror,* in Hartford, in 1817, and after his death in 1823, had come to the Troy Female Seminary with her two young daughters, Jane and Emma. She began teaching at once, and also studied French, Latin, and mathematics. Her love of teaching and her years of success in it before her marriage now served her well, as more and more work opened up for her at the Seminary. The two sisters, Emma and Almira, always drawn to each other by their love of study, worked well together, and Mrs. Willard grew very fond of Jane and Emma.

When Dr. Willard died on May 29, 1825, after a long illness, leaving Mrs. Willard with the full responsibility of the school, Almira was a great help and comfort. Dr. Willard had done his share of the work so quietly and unobtrusively, in such an orderly systematic manner, calling so little attention to himself, that few realized what a factor he had been in building up the school. He bequeathed to his wife all of his household furniture, all of his books, manuscripts, charts, maps, prints, paintings, pictures, musical instruments, and one third of his real and personal property. The copyrights of her geographies and her *Plan for Improving Female Education,* which he, as her husband, had owned, now under his will were turned over to her. The rest of his property was divided equally among his sons.

Mrs. Willard felt keenly the loss of his companionship and his help in the business management of the school. He had been so understanding and so sympathetic toward her work that she had instinctively turned to him for encouragement and advice. Her pupils, sensing her grief, presented her with a mourning ring, writing her, "Will our dear Instructress accept the enclosed as a pledge of the tender regard of her affectionate pupils?"

The amount of work to be done at the school carried her through this difficult experience. She took over a large share of Dr. Willard's duties, looking after the finances and keeping the books. The school property which had been leased to Dr. Willard, at a time when no married woman could make a contract or hold real estate in her own name, was now leased to her.

Her son's education also became wholly her responsibility, and she wrote the Speaker of the House of Representatives, asking him to obtain for John an appointment as a cadet at West Point. Through the efforts of several influential friends, including Governor Clinton, John was able to enter West Point within a year.

The opening of the Erie Canal in October, 1825, was a gala occasion for all the towns along the Canal and the Hudson River. By special invitation from Governor Clinton, Mrs. Willard and her pupils celebrated the event by a boat trip to "the nine locks."

The opening of the Canal meant a great deal to the Troy Female Seminary. It meant growth and an ever-widening opportunity for service, for all the newly opened Western territory could now more readily send its daughters to Troy for an education, while the Seminary in turn could send more teachers out through the West. Mrs. Willard, always an eager student of contemporary history, sensed its significance. East and West were being linked together. Now, throughout that wide expanse of wilderness included in the Louisiana Purchase of 1803, settlers would be pushing farther and farther west. The thirteen poverty-stricken, war-wracked colonies —which at the time of her birth in 1787, had been struggling to come to terms in the Constitutional Convention—had so developed and expanded that in 1825 the Republic of America was beginning to assume the proportions of a vast empire.

The Canal brought prosperity to Troy. Since 1820, Troy had more than doubled in population, and within three years after the opening of the Canal, had added three thousand to its population. Oil lamps now lighted its streets, door numbers were used to mark houses, River Street was paved. An "elegant and secure" steamboat, the *Chief Justice Marshall,* plied between Troy and New York two or three times a week, while not so many years before, the voyage had been made by sloop and often took a week, although sometimes with favorable winds the round trip had been made in four days. Robert Fulton's epoch-making trip up the Hudson from New York to Albany on his steamboat, the *Claremont,* in 1807, had so revolutionized river traffic, that by 1830 eighty-six steamboats were operating on the Hudson River. Stagecoaches made regular trips between Troy and Boston, and to Schenectady and Saratoga. Troy was in the hum of commercial development.

The Female Seminary also gave Troy a certain fame, and kept pace with the growth of the city, attracting pupils from every part of the country. When, in 1826, the growth of the Seminary made a larger building necessary, the city of Troy lengthened it forty feet

and increased the rent to $700 a year. In 1828, it became necessary
to erect an additional building; a few years later, more land was purchased and the main building was again enlarged. Mrs. Willard was
receiving a substantial income from the sale of her geographies and
was able to live very comfortably. In addition to *Universal Geography,* written in collaboration with William C. Woodbridge, she
had published in 1826, *Geography for Beginners or the Instructors
Assistant.*

Distinguished visitors came to the Seminary to investigate that
distinctly American experiment in female education. Commenting
upon the observations of one of these visitors, Mrs. Willard wrote
Maria Edgeworth: "An English traveller attended for a time upon
my last examination. He said to me, on leaving: 'Madam, you are
making a grand experiment here; we have nothing to compare with
it on our side of the water; but I fear you are educating girls too
highly; and that they will not be willing to marry.' But I have never
experienced any difficulty of this sort. The young men sought them
so resolutely for wives that I could not keep them for teachers."

For many years, Mrs. Willard had looked up to Maria Edgeworth not only because of the fame she had attained as an author,
but because she stood for the education of women in a country where
women's safety and virtue were considered synonymous with ignorance. Maria Edgeworth had proved that a woman could be well-
educated, succeed as an author, receive praise and adulation, and
still remain virtuous. It was only natural that Mrs. Willard's enthusiasm for such a woman should have led her to seek an exchange of
views on the subject of woman's education.

Mrs. Willard carried on a wide correspondence, never hesitat-
ing to enlist the interest of anyone whose influence might aid her
in her work or help her spread her message of higher education for
women. One of her correspondents was Elizah Burritt, an eminent
mathematician and astronomer, who was conducting a school
in New Britain, Connecticut. He first wrote Mrs. Willard about
enrolling his daughter in the Troy Female Seminary and
they continued to find subjects of mutual interest to discuss. His
Geography of the Heavens was later used as a textbook at the Seminary.

Mrs. Willard met the Minister to Colombia about this time, and through him sent Bolivar a copy of her *Plan for Improving Female Education* and a letter pleading for her sex, with the result that a female seminary was established in Bogotá. The influence of the Troy Female Seminary was gradually being felt throughout the world.

9 The Awakening
of American Women

Little did Mrs. Willard dream when she presented her *Plan for Improving Female Education* to the Legislature of New York in 1819 that, within ten years and without state aid, the cause of woman's education would forge ahead. The success of her Seminary in Troy had done much to change public opinion regarding the propriety of education for women, especially since her pupils emerged after several years of higher education as ladylike, if not more ladylike, than before they took up their studies and did not rush out into the world demanding to usurp man's sphere. In addition, the teachers sent out every year from the Seminary spread the message of woman's education in an everwidening circle.

The South was friendly toward the education of women, and it was there that at first the majority of Mrs. Willard's young teachers found positions. Southerners were not afraid to use the word *college* in connection with women's education. Elizabeth Academy in Old Washington, Mississippi, founded in 1817, was chartered as a college in 1819, but its course of study did not rank with that of later women's colleges. Dr. Elias Mark's Female Academy at Barhamville, South Carolina, established in 1815 and incorporated as a college in 1832, grew each year in numbers and influence. In Lexington, Kentucky, Lafayette Seminary, founded in 1821, shared the honors with the Troy Female Seminary in receiving a visit from Lafayette, and at that time, had one hundred thirty-five pupils and nine instructors. These schools, like the Troy Female Seminary, were introducing higher subjects and were working toward a standard of education for women more nearly equal to that for young men.

Although Mrs. Willard was the pioneer in advocating higher education for women, others were entering the field. Mary Lyon, in Massachusetts, was becoming known for her ability and zeal as a teacher. At Londonderry, New Hampshire—and then at Ipswich,

Massachusetts, with Zilpha P. Grant—she was experimenting, adding new subjects to the curriculum, and planting the seeds for her endowed seminary at Mount Holyoke.

In Hartford, Connecticut, in 1823, Catherine Beecher, with the aid of her sister, had opened a select school for fifteen young ladies in a room over a store. During the next few years, so many pupils flocked to her Seminary that she was obliged to call upon the prominent men of the city to raise money for the erection of a more adequate school building. Through the influence of the women of Hartford, this was accomplished, and the Hartford Female Seminary prospered, enrolling one hundred to two hundred pupils. Catherine Beecher, acting as principal with eight teachers to assist her, held yearly exhibitions to show what progress was being made. Her pupils wrote Latin compositions and translated Virgil and Ovid. Eventually every one of them studied geography, arithmetic, and grammar, although she found that most parents preferred a "finishing" school with superficial studies for their daughters. This convinced her that only schools with established reputations could introduce higher subjects. In 1829, she published *Suggestions on Education,* which was widely read and focused attention on the unequal education of men and women. She sent a copy to Mrs. Willard who wrote her: "Accept, my dear madam, my thanks for the able work which you had the goodness to send me. I have perused it with deep interest. Every effort to advance the cause it advocates has my best wishes for its success."

In 1826, the first public high schools for girls were established in Boston and New York. So great was the popularity of the Boston School that those opposed to women's education were alarmed and stirred up such feeling against it that it was closed two years later. The New York School was closed because it lacked an efficient head. Yet, in spite of critics and calamity criers, the cause of woman's education pressed steadily forward.

Education very naturally led women to seek opportunities for greater usefulness. A few found one in the antislavery movement then gaining momentum. In 1832, they organized Female Antislavery Societies, the first group attempt by women to take part in a reform movement. The Grimké sisters of South Carolina came North and soon began speaking against slavery, were ridiculed, and denounced, not so much because they were speaking against slavery, as because they were expressing themselves on a political question.

These efforts to take an active part in the antislavery movement made women realize how hampered they were by law and tradition. They were confronted by laws which held married women in complete subjection to their husbands, with no rights over their persons or children, no right to their earnings, no right to hold property, and so on. Out of attempts to amend these laws, the woman's rights movement was born.

Mrs. Willard was careful to take no part in any of these new movements. She made her attitude toward them plain in a letter, written in 1829 to Catherine Beecher, who asked her co-operation in a certain matter. "In reflecting on political subjects," she wrote, "my thoughts are apt to take this direction: the only natural government on earth is that of the family—the only natural sovereign, the husband and father. Other just governments are those sovereigns confederated. . . ." These sovereigns, according to Mrs. Willard, would consider the interference of women "unwanted officiousness" and would say, " 'The studies which you pursue have inflated and bewildered you; you are the worse for your knowledge; return to your ignorance.' " Then she added, "Such a sentence as this, my dear madam, you and I, as guardians of the interests of our sex's education, are alike desirous to avoid; and when the warm dictates of a generous benevolence shall have given place to sober reflection, I cannot but believe you will agree with me that we cannot, without endangering those interests, interfere with the affair in question."

Although abolition, temperance, and political subjects were taboo, American women were establishing themselves in the field of literature. *Moral Pieces in Prose and Verse* published in 1815 by Lydia Huntley of Hartford, later Mrs. Sigourney, aroused interest and favorable comment. This was but the beginning of her prolific outpouring of poetry and prose through which she won great popularity and the reputation of being the Hemans of America. Catherine Maria Sedgwick of Stockbridge, Massachusetts, encouraged by her brother to publish her *New England Tale,* became the outstanding woman novelist in America and her romances translated into foreign languages and reprinted in England, were more widely read in Europe than either Irving or Poe. In 1828, Mrs. Sarah Josepha Hale became the editor of the *American Ladies' Magazine,* published in Boston, and afterwards consolidated with Godey's *Lady's Book.* The aim of this magazine was "to recommend to the hearts and minds of American ladies, with the pursuit of intellectual and elegant accomplishments, the practice of every feminine duty and Christian excellence that can adorn and dignify the name of woman." In its pages, women were given the opportunity to plead for the education of their sex.

About this time, Mrs. Willard's sister, Almira Lincoln, fulfilled an ambition which she had cherished ever since she had heard of the publication of *Moral Pieces in Prose and Verse.* She published her first book. Teaching botany at the Troy Female Seminary, she had not found a textbook to suit her, so she decided to compile her own lectures and to publish them. Until then botany had been taught in very few schools, but the new textbook aroused such interest in the subject that in less than four years, ten thousand copies had been sold. For many years, Lincoln's *Botany* was the standard textbook in schools and colleges throughout the country. It was reprinted in England and translated into foreign languages. The critics of the day agreed with Mrs. Lincoln's introductory remarks that "the study of Botany seems peculiarly adapted to females; the objects of its investigation are beautiful and delicate; its pursuit leading to exercise in the open air is conducive to health and cheerfulness." Her *Botany* was followed by the publication of a *Dictionary of Chemistry,* translated from the French with additions.

Mrs. Willard had already become known as an "authoress" through the publication of her *Plan for Improving Female Education, Ancient Geography* and *Geography for Beginners.* Her *Republic of America,* published in 1828, gave full play to her powers. Her interest in history, so marked even in childhood, her great love for her native land, and her enthusiasm for the republican form of government, led her naturally to the writing of a history of her country. She dedicated *Republic of America* to her mother, Lydia Hart, in a poem fervid with sentiment:

> Accept this offering of a daughter's love,
> Dear, only, widowed parent; on whose brow

Time-honoured, have full eighty winters shed
The crown of wisdom.
                              Mother, few are left,
Like thee, who felt the fire of freedom's holy time
Pervade and purify the patriot breast.
Thou wert within thy country's shattered bark,
When, trusting Heaven, she rode the raging seas,
And braved with dauntless, death-defying front
The storm of war. With me retrace the scene,
Then view her peace, her wealth, her liberty, and fame:
And like the mariner, who gains the port
Almost unhoped-for, from the dangerous waves,
Thou canst rejoice:— and thankful praise to God
The Great Deliverer, which perchance I speak—
Thou, in thy pious heart, wilt deeply feel.

Republic of America began with a chapter on "Aboriginal In-
habitants of America" and continued through 1826. In place of a
Table of Contents, Mrs. Willard used an interesting chronological
chart, which was one of her original methods of teaching history.
Her suggestions to teachers in the Preface followed her plan of
teaching history at the Troy Female Seminary. Each pupil brought
her blackboard to class and drew on it from memory a map relating
to the lesson of the day, marking the paths of navigators and
explorers, and the march of armies. Then she explained her map.
Mrs. Willard felt it was useless to commit many dates to memory and
instead wished pupils to become familiar with the dates of epochs
and be able to group events accordingly. She suggested that they
connect events of history with the events of their own lives or their
families'. It was her theory that the more a pupil associated
his knowledge with himself the better he would remember it and
the more effectively he would use it in later life. Believing firmly
that "moral improvement is the true end of the intellectual," she
urged teachers to draw from the events of history such moral reflec-
tions as the events might suggest. The Constitution of the United
States, the Declaration of Independence, and Washington's Farewell Address were given in full in the appendix, because Mrs. Willard felt they should be studied by the youth of the country as their
"political scriptures."

Republic of America was hailed by educators, and newspapers reviewed it favorably, among them, the Boston *Traveler,* the Cincinnati *Gazette,* the United States *Gazette,* and the Albany *Evening Journal.* The *Traveler* commented: "We consider the work a remarkable one, in that it forms the best book for general reading and reference published, and at the same time has no equal, in our opinion, as a textbook. On this latter point, the profession which its author followed with such signal success rendered her peculiarly a fitting person to prepare a textbook. None but a practical teacher is capable of preparing a good school-book; and as woman has so much to do in forming our early character, why should her influence cease at the fireside—why not encourage her to exert her talents still in preparing school and other books for after years?"

The Ward School Teacher's Association of the City of New York called it "decidedly the best treatise on this interesting subject" and added: "The student will learn, by reading a few pages, how much reason he has to be proud of his country—of its institutions— of its founders—of its heroes and statesmen: and by such lessons are we not to hope that those who come after us will be instructed in their duties as citizens, and their obligations as patriots. Your committees are anxious to see this work extensively used in all the schools in the U. S."

A letter from Lafayette highly endorsed Mrs. Willard's account of the Revolutionary War. Daniel Webster wrote her: "I cannot better express my sense of the value of your history of the United States than by saying I keep it near me as a book of reference, accurate in facts and dates."

Such praise was very sweet to her for heretofore, like all pioneers, she had encountered more opposition and criticism than approval. To date only two other American women had ventured into the field of historical writing, the eccentric bluestocking, Hannah Adams, who in 1799 published her *History of New England,* and Mercy Warren, the patriot, who in 1805 published her very creditable *History of the Rise, Progress, and Termination of the American Revolution.* Since then the public had become accustomed to educated women so that a woman as an historian or the author of a textbook did not arouse instant disapproval.

Mrs. Willard's greatest satisfaction from the favorable acceptance of *Republic of America* was her realization that it could be of service to her beloved country. She hoped to see disproved the prophecies of European statesmen regarding the inevitable fall of the Republic of America, and instead to see the country steadfast, prosperous, true to its ideals, an object lesson to Europe. This could be accomplished, she felt, only by the proper education of America's youth, the barometer of future generations. It warmed her heart to think her book would inspire in the youth of America love of country and zeal for noble citizenship.

10   Days of Discovery in Paris

After sixteen years as principal of a rapidly developing female seminary, Mrs. Willard began to long for a rest. Year in and year out, she had 'been supervising and teaching, and studying during her free hours at night. With the added strain of Dr. Willard's illness and death, increased responsibilities, and intensive work on *Republic of America*, it now seemed wise to call a halt for a time.

A trip to Europe was something for which she had longed, but which had always seemed far in the future—a dream rather than a possibility. Now the more she thought of it, the more feasible it seemed. She could afford it, for the publication of her geography and history textbooks had made her financially independent. The Seminary was flourishing and could be left in charge of her sister, Almira, who had proved to be an admirable vice-principal. Such a journey, of course, could not properly be undertaken by a woman alone, but her son, John, now a young man of twenty, could accompany her. Although the trip would mean a break in his work at Washington College, Hartford, where he had enrolled after two years at West Point, it would be a rich educational experience for him. As she thought it all over, she began to feel that she owed it to her school and the cause of female education to investigate European educational methods. As a prominent American educator, she could travel with introductions which would assure her entrance into European educational circles. Lafayette's friendship would mean much to her in France. He had repeatedly urged her to visit his country. It was an opportunity not to be lost. She realized the dangers and uncertainties of ocean travel, and she was prepared. Her affairs were in order.

Before sailing, she fulfilled one last request of some of her pupils, who had written her: "Many of your affectionate pupils, expecting to leave you in a short time, not to return, and wishing to possess some memorial of your kindness and affection, as well as of the many happy days they have passed beneath your roof, anxiously request you to fulfill the promise made them that you would have the poems published which you were so good as to read for them in April, accompanied with an engraving of yourself, and which promise subsequent melancholy occurrencies in your family have as yet prevented you from fulfilling."

To this collection of poems, she gave the title, *The Fulfilment of a Promise; by Which Poems by Emma Willard Are Published, and Affectionately Inscribed to Her Past and Present Pupils.* Some critics ranked her poems with those of Mrs. Sigourney, but on the whole they were not well received. The first poem was a farewell to her pupils:

> My children! ye, whose minds are born of mine,
> Whose hearts beat toward me with a filial pulse,
> I leave you, so I deem God wills, and go,
> A wanderer o'er the main, to foreign lands.
> Ye weep as I depart. Your fancy swells
> The dangers of the deep, and ye are griev'd;—
> Grieved most of all, that ye on earth may see
> My face no more.
>   The world knows not how dear
> Ye are to me, and I to you, my daughters!
> . . . . Ye are to me
> The bodying forth of a long lov'd idea.
> I see in you the representatives
> Of future woman; of the cause I've served,
> Even with a martyr's zeal, and still will serve. . . .

She sailed for France with John on October 1, 1830, on the *Charlemagne,* one of the largest and fastest of the packets which were then the pride of New York. She shared the ladies' cabin with a little girl of eight, traveling alone from Philadelphia to Geneva where she was to be educated by her grandmother, and Miss D———, a young lady who was traveling with her father, and whom Mrs. Willard characterized as interesting, intelligent, and accomplished.

The trip was long and very rough, but Mrs. Willard enjoyed it all, even the dashing waves and rolling ship. She wrote her sister: "Yet I have not been sea-sick, neither have I exercised as much on deck, owing to the roughness of the weather, as I could have wished:

but the perpetual motion in which I am kept by the winds and waters; rocking, and rolling, and tossing; holding with might and main, by some fixed object during the day to keep from being shot across the cabin and grasping the side of my berth at night for fear of being rolled over the side—all this, though not particularly diverting at the time, is yet very conducive to my health; and seems to put in motion those vital functions, which want of suitable exercise for the body, or too much mental exercise had deranged."

She walked the deck on the arm of the stalwart captain, whom she imagined to be like Captain John Paul Jones, and with his assistance wrote a description of the ship, illustrated with drawings, which she sent to her pupils for their instruction. The sight of land, after the long voyage of twenty-four days, moved her deeply. "When I realized," she wrote, "that I was indeed beholding that ancient world of which I had so often strained my fancy to give me an idea —when I realized, that through a guardian Providence, my feet had escaped the dangers of the treacherous ocean, and stood again on the lap of my mother Earth—my joy was intense. I could have acted extravagances, but we belong to a race who seem cold because we suppress our feelings."

Landing at Havre, she began at once in her thorough manner to investigate everything and comment upon everything. She was as enthusiastic as a child about new experiences. The quaintness of the buildings, the dress of the peasants, the customs of the people fascinated her. She described the hotel in minute detail for her sister, from beds and candlesticks to table d'hote and the deafening racket made by Frenchmen in animated conversation during a meal.

On the long journey by diligence from Havre to Paris, through the countryside by moonlight and by day, she saw the moss-grown, thatched cottages of France and the ivy-covered walls about which she had so often read. The roses were in bloom; the fields were green. She was charmed by it all, and yet with truly American self-satisfaction, she considered "the scenery of France as much less interesting than that of America."

Paris was filled with innumerable delights and discoveries for her. The people, their customs, and their point of view interested her most of all. She went to the theater as much to see "the dresses of the French ladies and the general outward appearance of genteel

society" as to hear the celebrated actress, Madame Malibran. She
was impressed by the numbers of well-dressed women, by the beauty,
perfection and style of their gowns, by their charming manners. The
shops, public buildings, statues, art treasures, glimpses of royalty, and
drilling of the soldiers were some of the many things, aside from
politics and Lafayette, that kept her busy observing and philosophiz-
ing. She wrote long letters to her sister Almira and to her pupils,
letters typical of a teacher, written with an idea to instruct, but di-
mensions and plans of famous buildings, bits of history, and the
Puritanical viewpoint of an exemplary woman could not smother
her natural enthusiasm, insatiable curiosity, good humor, and refresh-
ing originality. She loved nothing better than a comment such as
this: "Here we see some of the greatest lions of Paris—lions literally,
couchant, on either side of the gate, which leads to the garden of the
Tuilleries. Fear not, but boldly advance; they have turned to stone,
or rather stone has turned to lions; and though they grin frightfully,
they are like many other 'lions in the way,' harmless to impede our
entrance."

Paris, however, meant first and foremost, Lafayette. Hearing
of her arrival, he immediately called upon her. She cherished every
moment of that meeting, writing her sister: "He met me affectionately. His heart seemed to expand as to a confidential sister,
and he talked to me freely of his family, and of the most important
political movements. He gave me a sketch of the Revolution—de-
tailed the part which he himself had taken—spoke of the present
state of affairs, and of the hopes and fears of the liberal party. . . .
His greatest regret was, that such was the state of public affairs, and
such his relation to them, that he had not the time he could wish to
devote to his personal friends. I repeated that those who loved him
best, would best know how to appreciate his situation. Yes, but he
spoke for himself. His friends might be better reconciled to all this
than he was.

"He enquired about his Troy acquaintances—spoke of you, my
dear sister, and of his young friends, my pupils—of the pleasure he
enjoyed there; of the beauty of the place. . . . His observations in
speaking of political affairs, were such as often gave to my patriotic
feelings a thrill of pleasure. He said . . . that he looked upon the

government of the United States as by far superior to any other existing. . . .

"He asked me if I had been to the House of Deputies. I had not. I must go—he would procure tickets, and one of his daughters would call for me the next morning. Do not, I beseech you, General, embarrass yourself about me. 'I will,' said he, 'embarrass myself about you; I will have that pleasure.' He then asked me if I had been to the Grand Opera. I had not . . . he would have the pleasure to go some evening with me. I did not utter a word, but bowed very low. I did not feel like speaking. I was deeply grateful for the honor he intended me.

"When the General had departed, I sat some time to recall his conversation, that it might not escape my memory. His discourse on the late revolution, and on the condition of France, is past and present history, drawn from its original source; for Lafayette, more than any other man of the present day, is making history for others to write, and for posterity to read." Even her wildest girlhood dreams had not anticipated such attention from Lafayette. Her cup of joy was running over.

The visit to the House of Deputies required preparation. Madame Maziau, her hostess, recommended a milliner who chose a becoming hat for her to wear on this momentous occasion. Lafayette's eldest daughter, Madame Latour de Maubourg, called for her, and spoke with pleasure of her father's reception at the Troy Female Seminary and of how many times they had sung the verses which Mrs. Willard had written and presented to them. From the gallery of the House of Deputies, they listened to the debates, watching for the arrival of Lafayette. After he had entered the Chamber and greeted his friends, his eyes searched the galleries until he discovered Mrs. Willard and his daughter. Then, he bowed three times. That afternoon, Mrs. Willard met another of Lafayette's daughters and was invited to attend his soirée. This invitation was repeated the next morning by Lafayette's daughter-in-law, Madame George Lafayette, who called and carried on an hour's animated conversation with Mrs. Willard in French. They were charmed with each other.

A few days later at half past eight in the evening, Mrs. Willard, regally clad, arrived at the soirée and was cordially received by General Lafayette and his family. She was introduced to Amelia Opie and James Fenimore Cooper, who with his family was spending some time in Paris. Of Mrs. Opie, Mrs. Willard wrote: "She attracts your notice, first among the crowd, from her Quaker costume, worn however with something of a modish air. She uses also the Quaker *thee* and *thou;* yet with her fine flow of thought, and occasionally ornamented style of expression, it can hardly be called the plain language. The other sex seem charmed with her conversation."

From social pleasures with the Lafayettes, Mrs. Willard turned again to sightseeing. Equipped with heavy leather shoes, she tramped sturdily over cobblestones and braved the French mud. One of her favorite haunts was the bridge of Louis XVI. She loved it especially for the twelve white marble statues placed along its sides, statues of warriors and statesmen of other days.

"I am so fascinated," she wrote, "by the marble society of this bridge, that I am in danger of running against something that I should not. . . . I am never tired of the acquaintance of these sages and veterans; and should I meet their shades, I am confident I should know them. . . . A people who erect statues to their great men, are more likely to know well, and intimately the history of their nation. And even strangers, sojourning among them, will better learn it."

She was gratified, too, that these statues were clad so as not "to offend the eye of modesty" and hoped that this was evidence that decency and propriety were coming into their own. The immodesty of statues in France was a continual source of distress to her. In a letter to her pupils describing the Garden of the Tuileries, she wrote, "No—my dear girls, I shall not take you to examine those statues. If your mothers were here, I would leave you sitting on these shaded benches, and conduct them through the walks, and they would return, and bid you depart for our own America; where the eye of modesty is not publicly affronted; and where virgin delicacy can walk abroad without a blush." The beauty of the Garden, she told them, might at first lead them to believe that they had found Paradise itself, but the expression on the faces of the crowds would quickly dispel that delusion. "Give me," she added, "for real, enduring happiness, the faces of the throng, who issue from the door of a New-

England church, rather than those of the crowds I meet in the Tuileries. . . ."

At the Louvre, where because of her great fondness for paintings, she expected to be sublimely uplifted, her pure womanhood was again affronted. However, she was willing to look for the wheat among the tares, to control her eyes and mind, and ignore what to her seemed vulgar. The Titians and the Raphaels at first disappointed her. The paintings of Girodet and the "wild sublimity" of Salvator Rosa roused her admiration. Those of the Italian school fascinated her, and kept drawing her back to them, until she knew she liked them best. Rubens was a great disappointment. "His works here," she wrote, "are full of faults, and the greatest of all are moral ones. . . . I am not ashamed to say, I have not visited the statuary. . . . I should rather be ashamed to say that I had."

Of Versailles, she wrote: "The world has but one Versailles, and it is to be hoped it will never have another. Men now understand too well their rights, and their strength, to allow one of their own number, again to fancy himself the state; and to use its united toil, and treasure, to uphold his personal vanity, and gratify his luxurious pleasures."

In Paris, whenever she crossed the Place Louis XV where the guillotine had stood, she cringed at the thought of the tragic days of the Revolution. It was not Marie Antoinette who came to her mind, but Charlotte Corday and Madame Roland's exclamation, "Oh, liberty, how many excesses are committed in thy name!"

The stormy history of France was much in her mind, for Lafayette had told her how the small Republican party, aroused by the oppressive measures of Charles X, had started an uprising and how he [Lafayette] had been placed at the head of the provisional government. It was his aim to conduct this revolution without needless executions and shedding of blood. "He would have preferred a republic," recorded Mrs. Willard, "but besides the odium which former excesses committed in this name had cast upon France, he knew that he should bring a host of foreign foes upon his country." He knew that the French were still monarchical at heart and not yet ready for a republic. In searching for a possible successor to Charles X, his thoughts turned to Louis Philippe, Duke of Orleans, who was known as a liberal. Assured that the Duke would support the principles of the Revolution, Lafayette agreed to make him king and promised, at his request, to remain at the head of the National Guard. For Emma Willard, the historian, it was a moving experience to be so close to events which promised to be the turning point in the political destinies of France.

She soon had the thrilling experience of attending the opera with Lafayette and his family, and sitting in a box next to that of King Louis Philippe: Lafayette had not attended the opera since the recent revolution, and hoping not to be recognized by the audience, he came in citizen's clothes and refused to sit in the front of the box. At his request, Mrs. Willard occupied one of the front seats. As she gazed out over the audience, she was dazzled by the beauty of the gowns and the splendor of the theater. She looked very lovely as she sat there, faultlessly gowned, her color heightened by the excitement of the evening. Animated, poised, a rare conversationalist, she easily took her place with the Lafayette family and their friends. Lafayette was delighted with her. The vigorous gray-haired hero, thirty years her senior, appreciated the Americanism which Emma Willard personified, that capable, intelligent, idealistic womanhood, which only America could produce.

"I observed that the eyes of the people were ever and anon, turning toward our box," reported Mrs. Willard, "and when at another interval we rose from our seats, as everybody did, suddenly there was a shout, 'Vive Lafayette! Vive Lafayette!' It sounded again and again, and was echoed and re-echoed by the vaulted roof. In the enthusiasm of the moment, I exclaimed, 'You are discovered—you must advance!'—and I handed him over the seats, unconscious at the moment that I was making myself part of the spectacle. He advanced, bowed thrice, and again retreated—but the cries continued. Then the people called out 'La Parisienne! La Parisienne!' " In answer to this, the curtain rose, and an actor, who had also been one of the heroes of the Revolution, sang "La Parisienne," the popular song of the Revolution of 1830. As he sang, he waved the tricolored flag, and when he sang the part which referred to Lafayette "with his white hairs, the hero of both worlds," the audience cheered. "I looked at him [Lafayette]" continued Mrs. Willard, "and met his eye. There was precisely the same expression as I marked, when we sung to him in Troy; and again I shared the sublime emotions of his soul, and again they overpowered my own. My lips quivered, and irrepressible tears started to my eyes. When the song was over, the actor came and opened the door of the box, and in his enthusiasm embraced him. 'You sang charmingly,' said Lafayette. 'Ah, General, you were here to hear me!' was the reply."

When Lafayette's party left the theater, the crowd lined a path for their hero. "There was that in this silent testimonial of their affection more touching than the noisy acclaim of their shouts," reported Mrs. Willard. "There was something, too, remarkable in the well-defined line which bounded the way left open. A dense crowd beyond—not even an intruding foot, within the space, which gratitude and veneration had marked. I can scarcely describe my own feelings. I was with him, whom from my infancy I had venerated as the best of men: whom for a long period of my life I had never hoped even to see in this world. Now I read with him his noble history, in the melting eyes of his ardent nation."

Mrs. Willard soon saw Paris on the verge of an uprising. During the trial of the ministers of Charles X, all sorts of rumors filled the air. The populace demanded a death sentence and feeling ran high. The Royalists expected a repetition of the bloody scenes of the former revolution, but there was hope that Lafayette could hold the mob in check. The family of one of the ministers, Mrs. Willard discovered, was in hiding in her boardinghouse. This and the knowledge that so much depended on her friend, Lafayette, made her feel very much a part of those critical days. When the sentence of life imprisonment was announced, the mob was infuriated. The soldiers threw down their arms in rage, shouting, "Vive la Republique! Vive LaFayette, notre President!" Urged to return to their posts out of loyalty to Lafayette, their commander-in-chief, they obeyed.

All that night and the next day the city was in an uproar. People thronged the streets. The entire National Guard was called out. From her boardinghouse window, Mrs. Willard anxiously watched the street, the men and women hurrying past, soldiers marching by. In her journal, she wrote: "We apprehended something dreadful; we hardly knew what. Towards evening we saw pass near our window, a great number of young men marching in regular files; with here and there an officer in the uniform of the national guards. They shout, but for a moment we know not what. They wear a placard in their hats; of this also we know not the meaning. They come nearer, and shout, 'Vive le Roi! Vive le Roi!' We see that their motto is, 'Liberte et l'ordre, Public, Public.' We breathe free, for we had feared that the multitude would prevail against the government. Soon after, we saw a numerous body of troops, their spears glittering by the light of the lamps. They shouted, and again we were all anxiety. At length we hear distinctly, 'Vive le Roi!' We waved our handkerchiefs from the windows as they passed; and in the joy of deliverance, hardly restrained ourselves from joining the shout. Candles were carried to the windows of the houses which they passed, to light the welcome band as they patrolled the streets. This was also a demonstration of rejoicing; and as such, the spirit was caught from house to house; and thus without any directions from authority, or preconcerted plan, Paris is illuminated. . . . All is becoming tranquil. Everyone we see praises the national guards, and declares that LaFayette has saved France from another revolution."

Then events followed which filled her with indignation. The King deliberately snubbed Lafayette by omitting to invite him to the review of the troops. The same day the King's party in the Chamber of Deputies abolished Lafayette's office of Commander-in-Chief of the National Guard. In Mrs. Willard's opinion, the Royalists feared the popularity of Lafayette.

"I have done with French politics," she commented with impatience, "and I have learned a good deal of French character; or rather of human nature. . . . The ill-disguised satisfaction of the royalists, the hypocritical pretenses of those, who wish to stand well on all sides, suit so ill with my feelings, that I now choose to keep silent, or retire when these events are made the topic of general conversation."

Many friends attended Lafayette's next soirée to express their affection and loyalty, as did Mrs. Willard, who recorded: "He appeared calm and benevolent as usual. Not the least touch of chagrin, or resentful feeling was visible in his appearance; but his countenance was to me as though he was struggling to overcome an inward sorrow, and wished not to be disturbed in this work of self-government."

Mrs. Willard had made many friends in Paris and had been so lavishly entertained that she wished to reciprocate by holding a soirée of her own, to which she invited seventy guests, among them General Lafayette and his family. "To be presiding lady of a fete in Paris," she confided to her sister, "gave me more feeling of wondering at the wonders, and most of all 'to see myself there' than anything else I have experienced."

At the request of General Lafayette, she had the honor of being presented at Court. In preparation, she consulted with Mrs. Rives, the Ambassador's wife, who told her that the more elegantly she was clothed, the more honored the Queen would be. There were some points which were not to be overlooked; her shoes must be of white satin, jewels must be worn, and her dress must be new. One of Lafayette's friends, Madame Z———, accompanied her to the presentation. Arriving at the entrance of the palace a little before half past eight in the evening, they gave their tippets to Madame Z———'s servant, and then passing between ranks of the King's liveried servants and the military guard, mounted a magnificent marble staircase at the top of which gentlemen at writing tables took their names and addresses and directed them to the main salon. Here they were joined by Mrs. Rives and the other American ladies who were to be presented. "Soon there was a movement in the upper end of the room," Mrs. Willard recorded in her diary, "and the Queen! The Queen! passed from lip to lip. She came forth elegantly, but not gorgeously attired; in blue, with a berri of white, with four white plumes. Instead of taking her stand, as I expected, at the head of the room, and there receiving severally, the ladies presented, she suffered us to keep our places and came to us. When she had arrived at our party, Mrs. Rives named to her the ladies one by one. She addressed some conversation to each. . . . When I was presented, she asked me how long since I had left my country, and remarked that I might if I chose, address her in English. I said I was charmed to find that I might speak in my native tongue, and be understood by her majesty. She said she did not speak it well, though she understood it. The King spoke it well; he was much attached to the Americans. I made her a complimentary reply;—she smiled, curtsied, and passed to the next. We had not space for any great flourish in our curtsies, but made them as respectfully as we might."

Soon after the Queen retired from the room, Mrs. Willard and Madame Z———— took their leave. "We promenaded the long halls of the Palais Royale with somewhat of a lighter step, republicans as we were, than that with which we had entered," she commented.

There were times when Emma Willard grew tired of the social whirl, when she roused herself with great effort to attend soirées and mingle in the gay life of Paris. "This is not the kind of life to make me happy," she observed. "Rather give me back my toils and cares, with the consciousness of living to a good and useful purpose; give me back too a society, whose conversation shall lead my mind to better things, than the toys of the world."

Always eager to improve her mind, she went to the College of France to hear Baron Cuvier deliver a lecture on natural history. It was just the subject she wished to hear, and as his enunciation was perfect, she understood his French very well. One of her objects in spending some time in Paris was to learn to speak French fluently. She found this more difficult than she anticipated because she did not wish to converse lamely in French at times when she ought to make a good impression. However, she did make noble attempts to speak French whenever possible, and took French lessons daily. Talking with the shopkeepers gave her excellent practice. She spent a great deal of time collecting books, prints, and paintings for her school, and bought a very up-to-date French wardrobe, not only to wear in Paris, but to take back to America with her. She hired French women to sew for her, and encouraged them to talk about their lives and customs, for she was eager to observe French character from all angles.

Next to meeting General Lafayette in Paris, Mrs. Willard had looked forward to calling on Madame Belloc. She presented her with a copy of her *Plan for Improving Female Education* and her *Poems,* and was pleased to learn that Madame Belloc had heard of her as a writer and was eager to read *Republic of America.* They soon became warm friends, drawn together by their enthusiasm for the advancement of women. They spent many happy hours to- gether and with Madame Belloc's very close friend, Mademoiselle Mongolfier, discussing the education of women. Mrs. Willard was soon calling them Louise and Adelaide. They were charmed with her. As Madame Belloc was a friend of Maria Edgeworth as well as the translator of her books, she gave Mrs. Willard a letter of introduction to her. Preserved in a notebook, yellow with age, is a copy of what would seem to be this letter: "Madame Belloc to Miss Edgeworth. She seems to me to be one of the most sane and complete minds one ever meets; a person of resolution, wit, heart, imagination—a union of beautiful and rare qualities."

Through the influence of Madame Belloc, General Lafayette, and James Fenimore Cooper, Mrs. Willard was able to visit many of the best schools of France. While they were all of interest to her, she found nothing which compared in any way with her Seminary in Troy. French schools, she felt, kept young women in a state of perpetual infancy, and instead of learning much from them, as she had expected, she found that she had many suggestions for them. She was convinced that French character would continue to be unstable until French women received a more solid and more suitable education.

At the institution, Cochin, she was much attracted to a bright, pretty eleven-year-old orphan with a remarkably sweet voice, and at once thought of taking her to America and educating her at the Seminary. The necessary arrangements were made and Pauline Gertrude de Fonteview became a protégé of Mrs. Willard. She also engaged a French teacher for the Seminary, a very pleasing young lady of good family, who with little Pauline met her later at Havre when she sailed for America. Pauline spent eight years at the Seminary where she became an accomplished musician.

Mrs. Willard's decision to leave Paris about the middle of April and spend some time in England and Scotland, made it impossible for her and her son to accept General Lafayette's invitation to visit him and his family at La Grange.

11   Impressions of England and Scotland

"In going from French to English ground, I had a feeling of getting home, among my own people, far beyond what I had expected," wrote Mrs. Willard in her journal. "The English language, after having so long listened to the French, was grateful to my ear." She felt this even on the steamboat, crossing the Channel, and when she first glimpsed the white cliffs of Dover, she was moved to poetry, jotting down these lines in her notebook:

> Hail Britain! hail thou island queen,
> That sits enthroned on yonder chalky cliffs,
> And stretchest far thy sceptre o're the main!
> Land of my fathers, hail! The vital stream
> Within my veins, true to its ancient source,
> Warms through my heart, as I approach thy shores.

In London she and her son took lodgings in a house where there were twenty or more regular boarders. She was pleased with the arrangement as it made it possible for her to become acquainted with English people and customs. Arriving during a renewed agitation for the Reform Bill, she found this subject the main topic in newspapers and in conversation. When King William IV expressed his approval of the bill by dissolving Parliament, a big public demonstration followed. London was illuminated and crowds thronged the streets. Mrs. Willard, her son, and several friends from her boarding house drove about the city in a carriage, admiring the brilliant lights, amused and yet frightened by the surging crowds, especially when they saw the mob hurling pennies through the unlighted windows of an anti-reformer's house.

Because the lower classes were impudent and the streets were not patrolled by military guards as in Paris, Mrs. Willard felt it unwise to walk about alone. However, in her thoroughgoing way, she saw all there was to see in London. St. Paul's Cathedral, she found sublime; and Westminster Abbey, although less magnificent than some of the Gothic cathedrals on the continent, she felt was more interesting to an American than any other spot on earth. "When I found myself in the poet's corner, surrounded by the almost 'animated busts,' and breathing statues of men, from whose spirits my own had drawn many of its best energies, I felt delighted," she wrote, "and I made it a point to pay my respects to the company, by addressing to each of them some of their own verses. . . ." In the Tower it was the armor that attracted her attention, especially that belonging to Joan of Arc. "It does seem to me," she reflected, "that our race must have degenerated in size and physical strength, since those days. I do not believe a modern lady could budge an inch with a weight equal to that of the armor of Joan of Arc."

In London as well as in Paris, Mrs. Willard met many celebrities. Soon after her arrival, she sent Maria Edgeworth the letter of introduction which Madame Belloc had given her, for there was no one in London whom she was more eager to see. Miss Edgeworth immediately invited her to spend the evening, and in a letter to her sister, Mrs. Willard described minutely this first meeting: "Miss Edgeworth is small but symmetrically formed, with not one single blue-stocking oddity about her. Her dress was ladylike—a delicate colored satin, with a turban—reminding me of that in the pictures of Madame de Staël. In her manners, there is nothing that marks the slightest consciousness of her superior powers. Attentive to please, she seems liberal of her fine conversation, and observant of little attentions to her guests. She appears more proud of her sister than herself; and remarked that she had educated her, and that while she had been writing those books which I had read, she was climbing her chair or pulling her papers. . . . There was a degree of intensity in my feelings toward Miss Edgeworth, of which I myself was hardly aware, until I saw her. I had long communed with her through her writings, and often wished to see and converse with her. . . ."

It was through Miss Edgeworth's influence that Mrs. Willard was able to visit some of the schools of England, but she received no more satisfaction from them than from those in France. Again she was astounded at the superiority of "female" education in America.

Washington Irving, who was in London in the spring of 1831, called on Mrs. Willard. Referring to him as "another of nature's nobles," she described their meeting to her sister: "As I had known and appreciated different members of his excellent family, our conversation took a turn which brought out his warm attachment to his friends and country. . . . He spoke too of his return to America. I told him that I presumed he was not ignorant, that we Americans were a little jealous of his long stay in Europe—regarding his literary fame as a national property, which we were unwilling should be alienated. He said nothing was farther from his intention than to remain abroad."

Mrs. Opie had given her a letter of introduction to Mrs. Elizabeth Fry, whose reform work in the English prisons was being discussed by all progressive women. "I felt a great interest in her favorite object, the reformation of prison discipline;—and she in mine—that of female education," she wrote her sister, "and we talked an hour in the full flow and mingling of soul."

She also met Robert Owen and in her conversation with him tried to avoid all controversial subjects. This proved to be impossible. "It is useless for you to wish me to agree with your views," she told him. "There is an insurmountable barrier. I am a Christian." When another member of the group declared that Christianity could be disproved in two minutes and Mr. Owen suggested that although a Christian now, Mrs. Willard might later change, she stood firm. "No sir," she retorted, "I never shall change. I never will change—a Christian I will live, and a Christian I will die."

When Robert Owen remarked that, of course, she would keep an open mind, she replied with firmness, "There is, Sir, a time to be investigating, and a time to be decided. When a mathematician has brought the best and maturest energies of his mind to bear upon a subject—when he has carefully attended to what others could say on both sides of the question—when he has thus perfectly satisfied his own mind where the truth lies; and when he finds that everything agrees to his solution of the problem—his operations on the supposition having never failed, his expectation never been deceived, —is he to go back, and labor through the whole process of his investigation, because he may find others who think differently from himself? No sir, I will not reinvestigate the evidences of Christianity—I shall never change my belief."

This silenced the discussion for a time, and then Mrs. Willard had the opportunity of discovering that Mr. Owen was well informed and very intelligent on the subject of education. He urged her to visit his school in Lanark when she went to Scotland.

The disparaging attitude of Englishmen toward America and Americans was a constant source of distress to her, for she was so completely convinced that her beloved country offered the world so much more than other nations. She was also amazed at the attitude of Englishmen toward women, at the way they talked down to them. "Englishmen," she said, "are afraid women will know too much, and consider that the perfection of our nature is to amuse them, or to do menial services for their convenience;—but for us to claim to be something in, and of ourselves—to think we have higher moral obligations than those we owe to their sex—to assert our equal right to intellectual cultivation;—this is all very shocking to an Englishman. There is a certain something in his manner when he addresses you, which makes you feel that you are a lady accosted by a gentleman,—a woman, spoken to by a man—one of nature's lords." For these reasons, she knew she would never be content to live in England. "My lot," she said, "is cast with my sex and country."

Leaving London, she and her son traveled by stagecoach and post chaise through Windsor, Oxford, Stratford, and Birmingham to Manchester. Between Manchester and Liverpool they had a thrilling experience, their first ride on that new invention, the railway. "At the appointed hour," recorded Mrs. Willard, "the cars set off, and the motion soon became fearfully rapid. The fields, the houses, and the trees seemed to fly to the east, as we sped on our westward course, scarcely giving us time to view them as they hurried on. The novelty of the scene would have delighted us, but for the feeling of danger which came strongly to us, as thus we were shot, by the power of steam, along these high embankments. Suddenly there was a terrific whiz, like that of a rocket when first let off; but louder. The first impression was, that something about the engine had gone wrong. We looked for an instant in each other's pale faces, and then at the strange appearance of an object, passing by our side, which seemed to present long horizontal lines of colors, while the whizzing noise grew yet louder. This was the train of cars from Liverpool passing with the apparent velocity of the two, which was about fifty miles an hour."

In Liverpool, Mrs. Willard was very happy to find a school for girls which more nearly met her standards. American textbooks were used, among them her own.

A boat trip from Liverpool took her to Scotland where memories of Scottish history were revived. Scenes from *The Lay of the Last Minstrel* and *The Lady of the Lake* passed through her mind, and she began to quote lines from her beloved Scott. At Lanark, she expressed approval of Robert Owen's experiment, noting the comfort and neatness of the workers' houses and the school which the factory children attended where they studied botany, music, and dancing, as well as the rudimental branches. "There certainly appears to be much to admire in the regulations here, which combine profitable industry, with physical and mental improvement," she commented.

Edinburgh fascinated her with its "wild and wonderful scenery," and the intelligence, wit, and warm affection of its people. She had never been so moved anywhere except at the tomb of Washington, for here were the graves of some of the fathers of her mind, as she expressed it. Although public schools for women had been sadly neglected throughout Scotland as well as in England and France, she found the general attitude toward women in Scotland more satisfying. "In Scotland," she said, "when men converse with you, you are permitted to feel that you are a human being, in communion with those of your kind."

After returning to London for a few days, she and John set out for Havre, with a young Englishwoman who had been engaged as a music teacher. Here they were joined by the French teacher and the eleven-year-old orphan, Pauline, who were to sail with them to America. They sailed about the middle of June after seven months in Europe. The voyage of forty-seven days was long, but very pleasant. Looking out over the vast expanse of water, Mrs. Willard felt her own utter helplessness, and turned constantly to God for protection. It was then that she wrote *Ocean Hymn*, better known as *Rocked in the Cradle of the Deep*, the one poem of hers that has lived. A fellow passenger, Count de Choiseul, set it to music, and during the rest of the voyage, it was sung as the evening hymn. Every evening as she joined in the singing, she felt assured of the truth of the words that had come to her so spontaneously:

> Rocked in the cradle of the deep,
> I lay me down in peace to sleep;
> Secure I rest upon the wave,
> For Thou, O Lord! hast power to save.
> I know Thou wilt not slight my call,
> For Thou dost mark the sparrow's fall;
> And calm and peaceful is my sleep,
> Rocked in the cradle of the deep.
>
> And such the trust that still were mine,
> Though stormy winds swept o'er the brine,
> Or, though the tempest's fiery breath
> Roused me from sleep to wreck and death,
> In ocean-cave, still safe with Thee,
> The germ of immortality!
> And calm and peaceful is my sleep,
> Rocked in the cradle of the deep.

12 Days of Prosperity and the Seminary in Greece

Early in August, 1831, Mrs. Willard was again presiding over the examinations at the Troy Female Seminary. The warm words of welcome, the admiring glances of teachers and pupils, the unpacking and displaying of treasures from the Old World, accounts of all that had passed at the Seminary during those long months when she was in Europe, all these things filled the first days of her homecoming with excitement and gratification.

"I well remember her arrival, and the joy with which she was greeted by the teachers and pupils who had known her before," recalled Elizabeth Cady Stanton, then a pupil at the Seminary. "She was a splendid-looking woman, then in her prime, and fully realized my idea of a queen. I doubt whether any royal personage in the Old World could have received her worshipers with more grace and dignity than did this far-famed daughter of the Republic."

Mrs. Willard was highly pleased with the progress of the Seminary during her absence. Her sister, Almira, had filled the office of principal as well as she herself could have done. She found, however, she would soon lose Almira's services through her marriage to Judge John Phelps of Guilford, Vermont. It was a happy marriage, for Judge Phelps was proud of his wife's love of study and literary ambition.

Mrs. Willard returned to her work with renewed vigor. Her Seminary had attained an unrivaled reputation, and was looked upon as the fashionable school of the country. More than one hundred boarders and two hundred day scholars were enrolled, while the number of teachers was correspondingly increased. As its income now greatly exceeded expenditures, financial problems no longer menaced its existence. The revised editions of *Republic of America* which Mrs. Willard called *History of the United States* had a tremendous sale, giving her a good income. In the words of a contemporary, "she lived in unusual style for a teacher, with beautiful pictures and treasures from the Old World in her parlors, with horses and carriages at her disposal, with many servants to look after her wants, with adoring teachers at her beck and call." Troy, then, was in its heyday, a little New York, bustling, making money, awed and impressed by wealth and position. Mrs. Willard met its standards. Troy was proud of her and of the Troy Female Seminary.

Since her return from Europe, Mrs. Willard had followed French styles in dress. "She was always robed—one must use the word 'robed,' so majestic was her bearing—in rich black silk or satin, and her head was crowned with a large white mull turban," reported Elizabeth Cady Stanton. "She had a finely developed figure, well shaped-head, classic features, most genial manners and a profound self-respect (a rare quality in woman) that gave her a dignity truly regal. . . ."

Admiration, fame, prosperity, all these were very dear to Emma Willard, and yet they were as nothing compared with her love for and devotion to the cause of woman's education. If she had her triumph—such as repeated requests from Europe for accounts of her work and lists of the textbooks used at the Seminary—she also knew disappointments and slights, as when George Barell Cheever published *The American Common-Place Book of Poetry with Occasional Notes* and omitted any mention of her work.

Superintending such a large institution as the Troy Female Seminary took a great deal of executive ability and wisdom, and there were days when Mrs. Willard felt "dragged from one thing to another from morning till night." Yet it had its compensations, such as the realization that she was truly serving her country by sending well-trained teachers to all parts of the United States. Reports from Catherine Beecher in Cincinnati emphasized the lack of schools and teachers in the West. Men, opening the wilderness, were far too busy to think about schools, and as a result a million and a half children were growing up in ignorance. Thirty thousand teachers were needed at once and ten thousand more each year to take care of the increasing population. This was women's first great opportunity to serve their country and they were able to respond because Emma Willard, Catherine Beecher, Mary Lyon, and other far-seeing pioneers had prepared the way.

During the summer of 1833, Mary Lyon, traveling to Philadelphia and Detroit, stopped in Troy to call on Mrs. Willard. At that time Mary Lyon had no definite plans for an endowed Seminary at Mt. Holyoke, but what she saw at the Troy Female Seminary encouraged and inspired her. Both women dreamed of establishing permanent educational institutions which would give to young women of moderate means the opportunities which only the daughters of the rich then enjoyed. With this in view, Mrs. Willard appealed unsuccessfully to influential citizens of Vermont to turn the University at Burlington, then in difficulties, into a female university supported by the state.

At this time she sent a copy of her *Plan for Improving Female Education* to Edward Everett of Boston, and fastened in the back of the booklet with a white ribbon, were several closely written pages telling of the progress of her Seminary. She warned that it was unwise to give too much power to boards of trustees and suggested that ways be devised "of so dividing the power of ultimate decision" that "evils resulting from their injudicious interference be obviated." She praised highly the Committee of Ladies which she had established.

Always interested in world affairs, Mrs. Willard watched with sympathy the struggle of the Greeks for independence from the Turks. Like all ardent Christians, she rejoiced in their triumph over a race of infidels. When in 1832, Greece became an independent state with Prince Otto of Bavaria as its King, Emma Willard began to plan for the women of Greece, hoping to bring them some of the improvements in education which she had given American women. Her plan was to establish a school in Athens which would train native teachers. Finding the Episcopal Board of Missions ready to co-operate, she set to work to raise money for the undertaking. Her first step was to interest the women of Troy. John Hill, representing the Mission Board and the clergymen of Troy, spoke at the first meeting. The response far exceeded her expectations.

She wrote a series of addresses on the *Advancement of Female Education,* the first of which was read in St. John's Church by Reverend Mr. Peck at a meeting of the Troy Society for the Advancement of Female Education in Greece. In this address, she pleaded eloquently for the Greeks and described her plans for helping them, adding, "In ancient story we are told that one of our sex remaining in Troy wrought harm to the Greeks. In modern recital may it be said, that women of American Troy have done them lasting good." This address and two others were published by the Troy Society and were widely circulated. Not only did they describe the deplorable conditions in Greece, but told of the progress of female education in America and the resulting benefits, stating more forcibly than ever before Mrs. Willard's opinions regarding the rights of women.

Through the efforts of Mrs. Sigourney, who wrote a poem to aid the cause, the ladies of Hartford became interested in the Seminary in Greece. From Boston, Mrs. Sarah J. Hale, editor of the *American Ladies' Magazine,* contributed an original hymn for the Troy meeting and offered to print Mrs. Willard's plea in her magazine, which was circulated in every state in the Union. Scarcely an issue of the magazine appeared in 1833 without some mention of the plan for furthering female education in Greece. Mrs. Phelps did much to aid the cause, and pupils of the Seminary aroused interest in New York, in Portland, Maine, and elsewhere. The sum of three thousand dollars was the goal, and Mrs. Willard, always ready with a practical suggestion, offered to publish her *Journal and Letters from France and Great Britain* and sell it at a dollar a volume for the benefit of the fund. The book was eagerly bought by her pupils and friends, who had been urging her to publish the story of her travels. The *American Ladies' Magazine* recommended it highly to its readers, commenting: "The letters are characterized by the playfulness and enthusiasm of a mind delighted with new impressions, and a naïveté which seems like the fresh glow of youthful feelings; but when she draws her deductions and enforces her principles, it is with the penetration of a philosopher, and the dignity of a Christian."

The *American Quarterly Review,* published in Philadelphia, felt differently about Mrs. Willard's *Journal and Letters.* In a long, sarcastic review, it ridiculed the book from beginning to end, criticizing the author for giving more lavish information about herself than about Europe. Its only kindly comment was the acknowledgment that her aspirations, views, and pursuits were of an elevated character.

Readers, however, delighted in the personal touch which the

American Quarterly Review so bitterly condemned. It was a new note in the formal, stilted style of the 1830's and the sale of this book alone provided a large portion of the fund for the Seminary in Greece.

The Greek Government publically expressed approval and appreciation of the Seminary established in Athens, and announced its intention of paying the tuition of twelve pupils. Dr. Samuel Gridley Howe, the American whose services in Greece won for him the title, "Lafayette of the Greek Revolution," wrote Mrs. Willard, "The members of your society, are, indeed, the friends of Greece, and deserve more of her gratitude than many who joined her in her struggle for independence."

Five hundred dollars a year was sent to the Seminary in Athens through the efforts of Mrs. Willard, until the Episcopal Board of Missions took over the entire control and financial support. Her interest in world affairs and causes such as this widened the outlook of her students. She did not keep them buried in their books, but roused in them an interest in international problems and a desire to work for the good of humanity.

13 Work and Play at the Troy Female Seminary

Interest in Greece did not keep Mrs. Willard from intensive work in her own school. Although she no longer taught regular classes, she was an indefatigable supervisor, training her teachers, introducing improved methods, and adding new subjects to the curriculum. It was physiology which now caused the greatest consternation among her critics. For women to study physiology was considered the height of indiscretion, robbing them of all delicacy. Mothers visiting a class at the Seminary in the early 1830's were so shocked at the sight of a pupil drawing a heart, arteries, and veins on a blackboard to explain the circulation of the blood that they left the room in shame and dismay. To preserve the modesty of the girls and spare them too frequent agitation, heavy paper was pasted over the pages in their textbooks which depicted the human body. Mrs. Willard was ready to make concessions such as these, but she would not allow criticism to interfere with what she felt ought to be taught, and in addition, she herself was interested in physiology.

She still considered the study of mathematics of prime importance because it would train women to think for themselves in an orderly way, help them to impersonalize their problems and solve them on the basis of abstract truth. Women, whose daily duties tended to make them look at everything from a personal angle and turn to others for ultimate decisions, must learn to reason and face a subject. Only mathematics, she felt, would give them this training.

As she considered correct English to be a mark of good education, she required a great deal of writing in every subject. Each week the girls wrote an original composition and copied it carefully in their neatest handwriting. Frequently, they were obliged to write out their translations to make them more polished and perfect than oral translations could ever hope to be. Shakespeare's dramas served as textbooks for oral reading. A teacher selected a play for her class to read and study, assigned a character to each pupil, and when the reading had been practiced in class until it was perfectly done, the play was read before the whole school to the delight of readers and audience. The youthful Portias, Shylocks, and Bassanios lived in an enchanting make-believe world for weeks, a wonderful bit of romance in the clocklike routine of the school.

Subjects were studied in groups. History of a given period was supplemented by geography and literature of the same period. For example, ancient history, ancient geography, and the *Iliad* were studied together. The pupils, of course, learned history by means of chronological charts which grouped historical matter in epochs, as this was Mrs. Willard's favorite method of teaching. In geography class they drew maps from memory to illustrate the salient points of the lesson.

The modern languages taught included Spanish and Italian as well as French and German. A few subjects were required—the Bible, composition, elocution, drawing, singing, gymnastics, and dancing. The higher studies were Latin, algebra, geometry, trigonometry, moral and natural philosophy, logic, botany, chemistry, geology, astronomy, zoology, natural theology, rhetoric, literature, and history. It was an imposing curriculum, not equaled by any other girls' school in the country in those years. Mrs. Willard's experience led her to observe: "The very pupils who excel most in those studies which men have been apt to think would unsex us, such as mathematics and natural philosophy, are the most apt to possess the elegant simplicity of truly fine manners, without mannerisms. Even personal beauty is advanced; for as a woman improves in taste, and as her will gains efficiency in every species of self-control, she rarely fails to improve herself in symmetry of form. . . . Genuine learning has ever been said to give polish to man; why then should it not bestow added charms on women?"

It was at examination time that Mrs. Willard showed off her girls and their accomplishments to her complete satisfaction. There were two public examinations during the year, one in February at the close of the first term and the annual examination which began the latter part of July and lasted for eight days. The annual examination drew crowds of spectators—parents, friends, and prominent educators, legislators, and clergymen. It was one of the great social events of the year for Troy and Albany. In the large examination room with its rows of ascending seats on two sides, the spectators gathered. They were seated on one side, while the excited girls, in white dresses with bright sashes, filed into the seats on the opposite side. Mrs. Willard, the examiners, and the various teachers whose classes were being questioned sat at a long, low table in the center of the room. Prominent educators were invited to be examiners and often they had never before seen young women prove problems in geometry nor heard them give analyses of Stewart's philosophy. Every class was examined thoroughly. The girls were questioned one by one, standing at the table as they recited, and usually two stood there together as this made it less embarrassing for them. Some of the best compositions were read, but never by the authors themselves, as this would have been too great a strain on the modesty of young ladies. Everything was done to keep girls from becoming too forward or bold.

The pupils always brought their blackboards and colored chalk with them into the examination room. The blackboards, two feet square, were easily carried under their arms. When the girls were examined in history or geography, they sat at the table in the center of the room, resting their blackboards against it, and drew map after map to illustrate what they had learned throughout the year. For example, the pupils who had studied Mrs. Willard's *History of the United States* were expected to draw from memory all the maps in the Atlas and a map for each year of the Revolutionary war; they were to recite the events of history and explain them with the help of their maps, and were to give an analysis of the Introduction of the textbook, of the Constitution of the United States, the Declaration of Independence, and Washington's Farewell Address.

The walls of the examination room were covered with pictures painted by the young ladies, an art exhibit very pleasing to the audience. Occasionally between recitations, a few of the pupils entertained the spectators by singing or playing on the harp or piano, and frequently the whole school joined in a song. Every day at the close of the session the pupils sang an appropriate hymn to emphasize the fact that it was the Creator who gave them minds capable of improve-

ment. The favorite hymn, sung with fervor at the end of the examinations, was one written by Mrs. Willard:

> O Thou, the First, the Last, the Best!
> To Thee the grateful song we raise,
> Convinced that all our works should be
> Begun and ended with Thy Praise. . . .

No marks, no medals, and no rewards were given at the examinations. To have recited admirably before such a distinguished audience was as great an honor as one could achieve. Contemporaries
who attended the examinations were amazed at the ability of the girls,
gratified to see them rosy-cheeked and healthy in spite of their ar-
duous mental labors, and pleased with their quiet and unassuming
manners.

Although the girls acquitted themselves nobly throughout the
long examinations, the weeks preceding were spent in agonizing over
them and cramming for them. Some wrote verses describing their
horrors. These by Lucretia Davidson were favorites:

> One frets and scolds, one laughs and cries,
> Another hopes, despairs, and sighs;
> Ask but the cause, and each replies,
> Next week's Examination.
>
> One bangs her books, then grasps them tight,
> And studies morning, noon, and night.
> As though she took some strange delight
> In these Examinations.
>
> The books are marked, defaced, and thumbed,
> Their brains with midnight tasks benumbed;
> Still all in one account is summed,
> Next week's Examination.
>
> Thus speed ye all, and may the smile
> Of approbation crown your toil,
> And Hope the anxious hours beguile
> Before Examination.

Although most of Emma Willard's pupils were studious, many
were also full of fun, always ready for a frolic, a bit of tomfoolery,

or a chance to break the rules. According to one student, there were three groups—the dulls, the romps, and the flirts. The dulls were always good and very studious; the romps played pranks and always planned some mischief; the flirts' chief interest was young men and the mark of membership in that group was waving a handkerchief from a Seminary window at some passing man. The sight of a Rensselaer-Polytechnic Institute boy caused many a heart to flutter. That was one of the compensations of the required daily walk, when the long line of girls, two by two, headed by a watchful teacher, tripped along the streets of Troy.

In the recreation plot at the rear of the school buildings, the girls vied with one another in the swings, enjoyed the seesaws in spite of impeding long, full skirts, and shrieked with delight and fear as they teetered high above the ground. Some played tag, others tossed bean bags, while the more sedate walked slowly arm in arm around the yard, exchanging confidences.

What a rush and a stampede there was for peanuts, molasses squares, and chocolate balls on Wednesday and Saturday afternoons when women with big baskets of goodies for sale gathered in the lower hall of the Seminary. After the plain meals, the frequent bread pudding, the plain bread which Mrs. Willard allowed between meals, baking day was a treat, and the four girls who served their turn in Cooking Class often lunched on applesauce and shortcake and took little cakes or pies to their rooms, much to the envy of their friends. The great achievement of Cooking Class was baking pies for Sunday's dinner.

From the music rooms where the girls were sent to practice, there often came strains of the "Russian March," "Napoleon Crossing the Rhine" or popular airs of the day, and it required a watchful music teacher to keep them at their lessons. There was great consternation among the guardians of the younger generation over the the popular songs of the day. That young ladies should express in singing sentiments which they would blush to utter in conversation caused their elders to sigh for the beautiful chaste songs of Mrs. Hemans.

After the annual examinations when most of the girls left the Seminary, the Southern and Western girls, who were far from home, often remained and continued their studies throughout the summer.

The work then was not so difficult, usually study and reading under the guidance of a teacher. They lived together like one big family, and evenings, when they gathered with their sewing, Mrs. Willard often read to them. *The Lay of the Last Minstrel* was her most frequent choice, for Scott was always her favorite author. To a remark that Scott was not a great poet, she replied with vehemence, "Scott not a great poet? As well might you say that a gun fired on the Alleghanies, that was heard upon the shores of the Atlantic and Pacific, was not a great gun, as to say that Scott, whose poems are read wherever the English language is spoken, and are translated into the languages of Europe, is not a great poet."

Mrs. Willard always kept a watchful eye on all the young teachers whom she had sent out into the world. In 1837, she organized the Willard Association for the Mutual Improvement of Female Teachers. She was its president and Madame Necker de Saussure, Madame Belloc, Mrs. Phelps, Mrs. Hale, and Mrs. Sigourney were among the honorary members. Not only did the Association aim to encourage teachers and help them improve their work; it also hoped by correspondence with them to gauge the actual state of female education and to learn what was promoting or retarding its progress in various parts of the country. By means of letters and addresses, Mrs. Willard made many sound, practical suggestions. She reminded young teachers that they could do more for their children in eight hours of healthful, active labor than in twelve of languid, sickly exertion. She warned them against overexertion, advising them to take time for exercise, mental recreation, regular meals, and sufficient sleep. She told them that in order to succeed they must always strive for self-improvement, and suggested teaching a new subject and studying at the same time. This, she felt, would develop independent methods of teaching and so interest the teachers that they could not fail to interest their pupils. They were to see that their pupils really understood their lessons and did not merely memorize. "Remember," she said, "that there is no special reverence for human opinions, because they are printed in a book." She emphasized the need of religious instruction. "Bring God into all subjects," she advised, adding that in so doing they would show His sway over all human affairs.

She was equally interested in the young women who married

and were bringing up children. She had found a book in France which she felt could be a useful guide for them, and with the help of Mrs. Phelps, she translated it. It was published in 1835. This book, *Progressive Education Commencing with the Infant,* written by Madame Necker de Saussure, the sister-in-law and biographer of Madame de Stäel, was widely circulated among the graduates of the Troy Female Seminary. In the Preface and notes, both Mrs. Willard and Mrs. Phelps freely expressed their own opinions. "Nothing can be more pleasing to the true friend of woman," commented Mrs. Willard, "than the sight of a well-educated female bringing all her faculties into exercise in the performance of the appropriate duties of her sex, as mistress of a household, as a wife and mother. To prepare the rising generation of women for these important duties, and to bring forward teachers to aid me in this, has been the grand object of my life."

Many of the book's theories are surprisingly like twentieth-century child psychology. For instance, Mrs. Willard stated in a footnote that she believed it wrong to break the will of a child, as will was the very stamina of the mind. Of course a child should be taught obedience and should know that his own wishes could not always be gratified, but this could be done in a manner which would not break his spirit. "Insult and ignominy," she wrote, "are heaped upon the defenseless being, as ungovernable passion or mistaken views of discipline may prompt, and either a sullen obstinacy, a morbid melancholy, or a servile abjectness of spirit, takes the place of that ingenuous frankness, that playfulness of disposition and noble independence which are so lovely and interesting in the young. . . ."

Her clear, penetrating, philosophical thinking is shown in another footnote: "It is certainly questionable how far we have a right to sacrifice ourselves. God has given to each of his great family the care of one being, that is, of himself—and if he neglect this one, or inflict upon him unnecessary pain, or deny him reasonable gratifications, is he not unfaithful to his trust? To *have right,* as well as to *do right,* seems to be the duty of each individual."

In 1837, another textbook by Mrs. Willard was published, *A System of Universal History in Perspective, Accompanied by an Atlas, Exhibiting Chronology in a Picture of Nations and Progres-*

sive Geography in a Series of Maps. In writing it, Mrs. Willard was again inspired with the desire to be of service to her country, to acquaint people with "the virtues which exalt nations and the vices which destroy them." She felt that the study of universal history was at that time peculiarly important to Americans, because the world was looking to them for the answer to this question: "Can the people govern themselves?" The next ten years would probably decide it for coming generations. "Shall monarchy in its palaces," she asked, "and aristocracy in its lordly halls, then exult, as it is told that America is passing through anarchy to despotism—while mankind at large mourn, and reproach us that we have sealed their doom as well as our own, and that of our posterity? Or shall we continue to be that people which of all others heretofore, or now existing, possess the most equitable government; and to whom national calamity is as but a phrase ill understood?"

While never so popular as her *History of the United States,* *Universal History* was nevertheless well received and highly endorsed by prominent educators. The Ward School Teachers Association of New York considered it "essentially adapted to higher classes of schools because of its vivacity, lucidness, and intelligent mode of arrangement."

Both books drew considerable attention to the Seminary, which received further publicity through articles printed in the *American Ladies' Magazine.* The September number, 1833, contained a short article on the Seminary by the editor, Sarah J. Hale, and an article by Mrs. Willard, entitled *Places of Education,* which pointed out that education is gained not only in the schoolroom but in every experience in life if the mind is alert and receptive. These articles were followed by pupils' contributions which, according to the editor, were printed to show their attainments in prose and poetry and their habits of thought and reflection. The frontispiece for the December, 1835, issue was a full-page picture of the Seminary, and a long article described the workings of that celebrated institution.

The *American Ladies' Magazine* also called the attention of its readers to the fact that already seventy-nine incorporated colleges and universities for men existed in the United States and not one single Protestant incorporated and endowed female seminary. "Men of America," it asked "shall this neglect of your daughters be perpetual?" Then followed the recommendation that the Troy Female Seminary, which had proved its usefulness, be incorporated and endowed so that it might be preserved for future generations.

The importance of the Troy Female Seminary was also empha-sized in a letter to Mrs. Willard, written in 1837, by George Combe, the renowned phrenologist, whom she had met on her European tour, and who had been interested in her work ever since the pub-lication of her *Plan for Improving Female Education*. "Your school is so extensive," he wrote, "and the influence of women on the state of society is, in my opinion, so important that I regard you as the most powerful individual at present acting on the condition of the American people of the next generation. . . . You may never live to see the good you are doing, but you may see it by faith."

Realizing her influence in the educational field and the respon-sibility which it conferred upon her, Mrs. Willard worked for the establishment of another institution for the education of young ladies —a school for teachers. This she hoped the New York Legislature would establish and endow, and she appealed to Governor Marcy. "You are aware, Sir," she wrote him, "that my views for the advance-ment of female education are connected with those I entertain of the improvement of common schools. Allow me here briefly to state my views. Common schools will never be well managed while there is a change of teachers every spring and fall—There should be settled teachers as in Academies. In a country presenting so many objects for enterprize as ours these cannot be men—Neither would men do so well (generally) as women properly qualified. Men are not happy as women are to spend their lives in communing with children nor can they teach the girls such handy works as they ought to learn in common schools, whereas women of talents may be prepared by education to teach boys all they need to learn even to the languages and the higher mathematics. It is a mistake to suppose that a woman of talents cannot govern lads of fifteen or sixteen years of age. The civil law I believe gives them the authority. . . . But these women must, in order to be properly qualified to teach and to govern, first be educated themselves and they must be paid not one dollar a week but about $250 pr. annum. They can get more than that sum to go to the south and west. Another object connected with the improve-ment in female education is the amelioration of the condition of those hundreds of young women who are labouring like mill-horse drudges in factories though many of them are the daughters of those who achieved our Revolution, and those who are to be the mothers of the next generation. Schools organized on a peculiar plan and allowing such of those young women who are disposed to learn to spend half or one third of their time in learning should, I think, be made for their benefit in the vicinity of great factories. This would elicit the talent there is among them and the first-rate scholars might be taken and educated as teachers of common schools—and this brings us back to the starting point that there must be a right place to teach these teachers."

While Mrs. Willard was evolving these plans for the education of women and was trying once more to interest a governor and a legislature, Mary Lyon was putting her heart and soul into plans for an endowed, permanent seminary for women. Addressing public meetings, collecting contributions in her little green bag, going from door to door and from town to town, urging men and women to make an investment for the education of their daughters, Mary Lyon was able to raise more than $27,000. She explained her project by referring to the Troy Female Seminary, Miss Beecher's Seminary at Hartford, and her own work at Ipswich. She did not have to argue for woman's mental capacity. Emma Willard had proved that. Mary Lyon's plea was for a permanent institution with lower tuition. The seminary was to bring education to poorer girls. On November 8, 1837, before the new school building was completely finished or furnished, Mount Holyoke Female Seminary at South Hadley received its first pupils. At first its course of study was similar to that of the Troy Female Seminary, except that it included none of the ornamental branches. Mount Holyoke, however, had entrance requirements and a regular three-year course, while Troy Female Seminary with no entrance requirements, admitted pupils at any time on the condition that they attend the examinations at the end of the term, and awarded diplomas to pupils who had creditably passed examinations in the full course of English studies with Latin or one modern language.

Meanwhile, other educational institutions had opened their doors to women. The Oberlin Collegiate Institute, founded in 1833, in Ohio, admitted men and women, black and white. The female department gave instruction "in the useful branches taught in the best female seminaries," but higher classes of the female department were given the privilege of attending some of the higher departments of the institute, best suited to "their sex and prospective employment." Wheaton Seminary, founded in 1834 in Norton, Massachusetts, by Judge Wheaton in memory of his daughter and at the instigation of his daughter-in-law, was patterned after Mary Lyon's Ispwich Seminary. Endowed with $20,000 to be used for the cause of education and guided by the progressive advice of Mary Lyon, it became an important institution for women.

Emma Willard had the satisfaction of seeing women's education accepted and supported in the East and in the West, in the North and in the South, and taking strides toward college education.

14   Return to Connecticut

It was a great satisfaction to Emma Willard to look back and think over all that she had accomplished. She had built up a successful school without state aid. She had proved that women were capable of mastering collegiate studies and were unspoiled by them. She had sent hundreds of teachers out from the Seminary and they were bringing education to an ever-increasing number of American girls. Her textbooks were being used throughout the country.

Now that the constructive pioneering work was done, she felt more and more like turning over to others the management of the Seminary. She was eager for new fields which would widen her sphere of usefulness and put into play her independent methods of investigation and organization. The training of teachers and the writing of textbooks had become her chief interests, for through them she could reach the common schools and the minds of hundreds of readers.

In a sense, the Seminary had come to a standstill. The city of Troy had, in 1837, turned over enough property to the trustees to make the Seminary eligible for a portion of the State Literature Fund. This was the first state aid that Mrs. Willard received for her school. Every attempt to obtain an endowment which would insure permanency for the Seminary had so far proved futile, and a real college for women still seemed out of reach. All that was necessary now was an alert, intelligent manager who would uphold present standards. This manager, Mrs. Willard had at hand in her daughter-in-law, for John had married one of her pupils, Sarah Lucretia Hudson, who had begun teaching at the Seminary when she was sixteen and had become vice-principal at twenty-one. After their marriage in 1834, John had taken over the business management of the Seminary and Lucretia had continued as vice-principal.

It was during these years when the Seminary was ceasing to be an all-absorbing interest that Mrs. Willard made the acquaintance of Dr. Christopher Yates, a physician of Albany and New York. She married him in September, 1838, leaving the Seminary in charge of John and Lucretia who became Principal.

Emma Willard's second marriage proved to be very unsuitable and unhappy. Fortunately, she had had the wisdom to draw up a marriage agreement by means of which she retained a hold on her property, for in those days, under the law, a wife's property at once became her husband's. This marriage agreement protected the Troy Female Seminary and the future of her son.

They lived in Boston for a time, but in June, 1839, after nine months of disillusionment, Mrs. Willard left Dr. Yates and returned to Connecticut to live for a time with her sister, Mary Lee, in Berlin, where in the peace of the countryside, she hoped to be able to pick up the broken threads of her life. In 1843, her marriage was dissolved by the Connecticut Legislature, and she was given the right to use the name Emma Willard. It had taken a great deal of courage to consider divorce by legislative enactment, the only possible way at that time. She realized only too well that a divorced woman was regarded as a social outcast and would be blamed for leaving her husband no matter what his faults might be. She, who so highly respected convention, now found herself in a humiliating situation. "I am now like a mariner who has escaped shipwreck," she wrote, "thankful for what is saved—for life, for reason, friends, and a thousand comforts with which kind Providence has surrounded me."

To occupy her mind, she returned to her study of science and physiology and began to write an essay on *Respiration and Motive Power.* She took long leisurely drives in the country. For the first time in many years, she lived close to the beauty of nature. The brilliant foliage of autumn, the clusters of wild purple asters, and cornfields bright with pumpkins brought back memories of happy October days in Middlebury. The bustle of the busy harvest season soon cast its spell over her, and her old eagerness for work returned. Then came the opportunity to help Henry Barnard build up the common schools of Connecticut.

Mrs. Willard had met Henry Barnard through their mutual friend, Dr. Eli Todd of Hartford, who had inspired them both with his interest in education, his enthusiasm for Pestalozzi, and his work for more humane treatment of the insane. After graduating from Yale and preparing for the practice of law, Henry Barnard had spent several years in Europe studying social, educational, and political conditions. When he returned to this country, he was elected to the Connecticut Legislature where he engineered the passage of a bill which would enable him to improve the schools of his native state. Investigations had revealed that from six to eight thousand children did not attend school, that only three hundred of the twelve hundred schoolhouses were fit to be used, that there were no fixed standards for teachers, no examinations to test their ability to teach, that two hundred varieties of textbooks were in use. People of wealth and influence sent their children to private schools, and as a result the common schools had been outrageously neglected. In order to remedy this, it was necessary to rouse the mass of the people out of their apathy, and as Secretary of the State Board of Commissioners for the Common Schools, Henry Barnard traveled throughout Connecticut holding meetings to explain actual conditions and urge a reform.

For one of these meetings, Henry Barnard asked Mrs. Willard to write an address. This she did gladly, but as it would have put too great a strain on the proprieties for a woman to read her own address before such a mixed audience, Elihu Burritt read it for her, and according to reports, it was listened to "with deep and thrilling interest." In fact, so telling was Mrs. Willard's plea for education that a committee of leading citizens asked her to take charge of the four schools of the district, and shortly after, the voters of Kensington elected her Superintendent of the Common Schools, "to take oversight of them for the ensuing season." She accepted on the condition that the women of Kensington support her in her work, and to show that she was willing to contribute her share in money toward improving the schools, she offered to pay a school tax equal to that paid by the wealthiest member of the community.

She took up the work with her old enthusiasm. As the schools were convening in May for their summer session, a "female" teacher had been placed in charge of each one, and older pupils chosen to assist them in their work with the younger children. While Mrs. Willard would have preferred a regular corps of well-trained teachers, she knew this was impossible on account of the expense. Pupil-teachers could help out very well as they had for so many years at the Troy Female Seminary.

"Each school house," she wrote Mr. Barnard, "should we think be provided with a clock; no matter how plain, if it do but perform its office correctly. Whatever is to be done regularly requires a set time as well as a fixed place; and teachers on low wages cannot afford to buy watches; nor would they serve the purpose of a perpetual momento of the coming duty of the scholar, like a clock."

Grieved at the amount of fiction that had been put in the hands of the children, she selected new textbooks. "Fiction," she explained to Mr. Barnard, "may mislead, even when it intends to do good—truth never. . . . In general, sacred objects are the best for schools. There is even among children, an awe and quietness diffused by ideas pertaining to God and religion, which tend to good order; and shed around the true atmosphere of the soul."

She drilled the children in reading, in geography, and arithmetic, paid special attention to their penmanship and spelling, dictated model business and social letters, and encouraged the writing of compositions. Finding that many children under ten had not learned to write, she set to work to remedy this and kept them busy with their slates and at the blackboard. "When the little children found that they themselves could produce the written language," she wrote Mr. Barnard, "it seemed to give them the most vivid delight; and instead of manifesting the reluctance to composition which older scholars almost invariably have, they were troublesome with bringing me their little compositions. This experiment has convinced me of what I before expected, that the unconquerable distaste for composition which is found in schools by older pupils, arises from our passing by the proper period of early childhood, before we begin to teach the communication of ideas by writing."

Another fault which she was eager to correct was toning, that monotonous unintelligent manner of reading which was so common in the schools of that day. Nor would she let the children memorize the answers to questions, but tried to have them gain a general knowledge of every subject they studied. "What we wish to effect," she wrote Mr. Barnard, "is not so much to give our schools a few facts from books, as to give them the power of using books to profit."

She taught the children Bible history, supervised their music, wrote a song for them, "Good Old Kensington," which they loved to sing, and a simple prayer which they recited at the close of each session. She offered a prize to the girl who could make the best shirt, for in her opinion the making of a shirt had from time immemorial been the test of good common sewing. She introduced a normal class for those who were planning to become teachers and for those who assisted in teaching the younger pupils, and in this work, she found an able helper in her niece, Harriet Hart, who had been trained at the Troy Female Seminary. She held classes for the teachers on alternate Saturdays, instructing them in history, reading, algebra, geometry, and in methods of teaching. So interested was she in her work that she talked to everyone about it and organized a "Female Common School Association" among the women of Kensington. Her address to them, *The Relation of Females and Mothers Especially to the Cause of Common School Improvement* was printed in Henry Barnard's *Connecticut Common School Journal,* as were many of her addresses and suggestions regarding the schools. This address received notice outside of Connecticut and was read before the annual meeting of the Western College of Teachers at Cincinnati, Ohio. In fact, Mrs. Willard's work in the common schools of Kensington was looked upon as a model for improving schools throughout the country. Many educational and literary societies asked her to meet with them to tell them of her work, those at a distance requesting her to write addresses for them.

The public examination, which she had found so useful in the Troy Female Seminary, she introduced into the Kensington schools. The first one, held at the Congregational church in September, 1840, was a gala occasion, attended by parents and prominent educators from all parts of Connecticut and even from other states. Although the exercises commenced soon after nine in the morning and continued with but an hour's intermission until six-thirty at night, contemporaries reported that there was "no abatement of interest in the audience or weariness in the children."

Meanwhile Henry Barnard had become a national figure in the field of education. Through his *Journal,* he expressed his constructive ideas in education and described the development of Connecticut's common schools. He was in constant demand as a lecturer throughout the country. Horace Mann called upon him again and again to speak for the cause in Massachusetts and their work helped to make possible the founding in Massachusetts in 1838 of the first state-supported normal school in the country. Mr. Barnard's Teachers Institute, held in Hartford in 1839 for six weeks, with daily class instruction, did much to arouse interest in a normal school for Connecticut and Mrs. Willard was regarded as the logical head of such an institution.

"There is a desire manifested by Mr. Barnard, and others," she wrote at this time to her cousin, Nancy Hinsdale, "that I should go to the head of a school for teaching teachers for the common schools, and the proposition has been, this last week, taking some form and shape. . . ." She told of a large brick building in Hartford which was being considered for the school. It was occupied in part as an orphanage, but as she wanted a model school for her teachers, she was delighted at the prospect of conducting the orphanage and normal school simultaneously. The orphans, she felt, would make exceptional pupils for a model school as there would be no unreasonable parents at hand to interfere. Her idea was to have a series of Teachers Institutes rather than a permanent normal school, with two sessions of four weeks each, held when teachers could attend without giving up their positions. Students were to enroll for four successive sessions and complete the prescribed course of study. This type of normal school, she felt, would reach more of the men and women then actively engaged in teaching and would therefore bring more immediate good to the schools of the State.

Hearing of her plans, her son wrote to dissuade her, urging her to come to Troy and live in her little house on the Seminary grounds, where she could observe and advise and devote herself to writing. As it happened, the proposed Hartford Normal School did not materialize, for political changes in the State temporarily terminated Henry Barnard's work and influence there.

At that time the girls working in the Lowell, Massachusetts, mills were attracting attention through their magazine, *The Lowell Offering*, and Mrs. Willard, always heartened by every effort by women for education and self-improvement, read it with great satisfaction. An editorial in the June, 1843, number, advocating a Manual Labor School, was of particular interest to her. It suggested employing one set of girls in the mills in the morning and another set in the afternoon, giving each girl six hours of mill work, three hours of study, and three hours of housework, a twelve-hour day being then a matter of course. She, herself, had suggested a similar plan to Governor Marcy of New York in 1836. Now she sent an approving letter to the editor of *The Lowell Offering* which was published September, 1843. "Such a plan of Manual Labor School," she wrote, "I fully believe to be practical. I should sincerely rejoice to see it carried into effect. . . . That Manufacturers would find it to their interest to encourage such schools, I also believe. . . . Let them follow up this system to its perfection, and endeavor to rear up a set of women ennobled by science as well as by usefulness and virtue; and then the good and respectable will more and more be content to serve them, while more and more they will secure their own interests, and at the same time those of patriotism and philanthropy."

Her next interest developed in Philadelphia where she spent some time conferring with her publisher, A. S. Barnes, and revising her histories. She seriously considered making her home there and editing an educational journal to be called *The School Mistress*. Her sister, Almira Phelps, advised against it. She warned her that she must not count on making money and that many such papers had failed. Mrs. Phelps was then living in Ellicott's Mills, Maryland, where she and Judge Phelps had taken charge of the Patapsco Institute, an Episcopal School for young ladies. "The idea of the periodical," Mrs. Phelps wrote her, "I should like very well on my own account, and might sometimes give you aid. If Mrs. Hale, Miss Leslie, and yourself could write, you might do something popular and useful at the same time; yet again there are so many jealousies among literary ladies that you might not get on well, even if you could be agreed enough to begin."

The plan was given up, and in the summer of 1844, Mrs. Willard returned to Troy as her son had urged her to do.

15 Calling Women to the Common Schools

In the little red-brick house on the corner of the Seminary grounds, Mrs. Willard spent many happy years. She could look out from her windows, across her well-kept garden to the Seminary. Her vigorous personality still dominated its policies. The Seminary catalogue now read: "The Founder of the Institution, Mrs. Emma Willard, has her residence on the Seminary grounds, and is at all times ready to extend to its members the results of her successful experience as an educator." She loved all of the Seminary's ever-changing family and shared their interests, affectionately calling this generation of girls her "granddaughters." In a trailing black satin or velvet gown, with soft creamy lace neck-ruff and hand ruffles, and a lacy headdress which set off her gray curls, she was the commanding figure at all their entertainments and at the annual examination. Her presence in the dining room for Sunday dinner roused a flutter of excitement. She, in turn, was stimulated by the pupils' adulation, happy to be among those who loved and respected her. Like all grandmothers, she was proud and pleased over John's and Lucretia's family of five children. Her favorite niece, Jane Lincoln, lived with her as companion and secretary, and often other nieces and relatives temporarily made their home with her. In fact, she was always surrounded by a bevy of young relatives who were being educated at the Seminary.

The Seminary girls were welcome at the little red-brick house. Mrs. Willard was at home to them on special days, and when two or three of them shared a simple meal with her, as they frequently did, she entertained them as if they were distinguished visitors, eager to interest them and to encourage them to express themselves on serious subjects. She stayed young with them, and they loved her and knew she was their friend, although they remained in awe of her. She longed to keep them improving their minds when they left the Seminary, and urged a teacher's career as the height of useful service. Quoting Dr. Thomas H. Gallaudet, an educator well-known for his work with the deaf and dumb, she advocated one or two years of teaching in the common schools for every woman who was a friend of her country. "If you do not teach, yourself," she often told them, "pass not by unnoticed the teacher. . . . Seek her out and help to give her a standing in society that may make her respected by herself and her pupils. Visit her in her school, and then, between yourself and her, give her any hints that you see she needs; and why not take an hour a day, if this too is needed, in helping her to teach?"

Again and again, she repeated to the girls the remarks of foreign statesmen who feared for the stability of the country's democratic institutions, and who said, "If America is saved, it is her women that must save her." She did her best to prepare them for this task and urged them to be studious, steady, and intelligent, avoiding vain amusements and the snares and follies of luxury. Always, she urged self-improvement and sensing the temptation that befell young mothers to give up everything for the routine work of caring for home and children, she wrote her niece, Emma Lincoln O'Brien: "I hope you will not drop your pen, and shut up your piano, and make your education of no avail because you have a child. A little extra resolution is needed to find or make time, but that is all that is necessary. Mrs. John Willard, with five children, performs well the duties of principal of this school."

Emma Willard, herself, had in no sense retired from active work. She was in constant demand as an adviser, teacher, and speaker in the educational revival taking place in New York State. Her first invitation came from the County Superintendents of Common Schools who held a convention in Syracuse in the spring of 1845. She was made an honorary member of their association and was asked to take part in their public debates. She went to Syracuse, but instead of speaking at the convention, she followed the more lady-like procedure of allowing sixty of the gentlemen to call upon her at which time she read them an address she had prepared for the occasion. In it, she mapped out the place which women should hold in the common schools, recommending especially the formation in every town of a society of women to co-operate with men in improving the schools. Her address was published in the newspapers and in the common-school journals, and as a result, she was asked to make a tour of several counties in southern New York to attend teachers' institutes. She set out in September, in her own carriage with a companion, one of her former pupils, spending a week in Monticello where she taught a hundred teachers, men and women, and persuaded the men of the town to invite the women to form an educational society. She was gratified to hear later that the men had given the women fifty dollars with which they had clothed some poor children and sent them to school.

Driving on to Binghamton, Owego, Cairo, and Rome, she conducted similar teachers' institutes, traveling seven hundred miles and instructing as many as five hundred teachers. In all her educational work, she stressed the importance of employing teachers who were more or less permanent in the profession, as children could not be expected to progress rapidly when they were given new teachers every few months. She maintained that women were especially suited to the profession, and unlike men, were willing to spend the greater part of their lives with children, training and guiding them. She also advocated more adequate salaries for teachers.

An unexpected opportunity for a trip through the West soon presented itself, and she wrote Mrs. Sigourney how it all came about: "When I wrote you last I had no thought of making this long journey but one day soon after, my son having been looking over our demands against many persons in different parts of the Union said to me, 'We must send out an agent and such a person will go if I wish it.' 'Why,' said I, 'if we must be at this expense should I not go myself? I have long had the intention to make a tour of the U. S.' 'Most assuredly,' said John, 'if you will go—but talking of going won't answer.' 'Well give me twenty hours to consider.' Then I called Jenny Lincoln and on my asking her how she would like such a tour, her face lightened and her eyes sparkled with pleasure. This decided me."

Mrs. Willard's journey of eight thousand miles through the South and West with her niece, Jane Lincoln, was by stagecoach, packet, and canalboat, and often by private carriage, as no railroad yet connected the West with the East. She visited all the principal cities in every state, west and south of New York, with the exception of Florida, Texas, and the Far West. It was a triumphal tour, as former pupils, in every part of the country, welcomed, entertained, and honored her. Her reception in the South was especially gratifying for here the majority of her pupils lived, many of them the belles of society, many of them teachers in southern Seminaries. Traveling through Arkansas, Missouri, Iowa, and Wisconsin, she found even there, close to the frontier, her "daughters" and her teachers. At all the Seminaries which she visited, she was looked up to as a pioneer educator, as the woman to whom they owed their existence. Everywhere, she answered questions and gave advice. Everywhere, she urged women to take an interest in the common schools. Like Henry Barnard on his nation-wide lecture tours, she left behind her a zeal for more and better schools and roused in women a will to assume responsibility for education.

When she returned from this long journey, she found waiting for her an invitation from the County Superintendents of New York to attend their meeting in Glens Falls. As she had been injured in the overturning of a stagecoach in Ohio, she was unable to accept, but wrote a long letter to be read at the meeting, calling women to the common schools. "If the men, amidst their many occupations," she wrote them, "have not more time to command, there are educated women who have, and who would be honored and their minds made more active and comprehensive, by serving under the superintendents on various committees connected with the welfare of the schools. I do not wish women to act out of their sphere; but it is time that modern improvement should reach their case and enlarge their sphere, from the walls of their own houses to the limits of the school district. In the use of the pen, women have entered the arena, and if we take all the books which are now published, I believe those which well affect the morals of society are, the one-half of them, the works of women; but, in the use of the living voice, women are generally considered as being properly restricted to conversation. St. Paul has said they must not speak in churches, but he has nowhere said they must not speak in school houses. To men is given the duty of providing for children, to women that of applying to their use this provision; and why should not the men and women in school-districts meet together for discussion? . . . These suggestions may now sound strange, as they foreshadow a new shade of things. But

I see it in the future, and rejoice in it as the harbinger of a brighter moral day than the world has yet seen. . . ."

In addition to all these tasks, Mrs. Willard had published several textbooks. *Temple of Time, or Chronographer of Universal History,* 1844, was followed by *Chronographer of English History, Chronographer of Ancient History,* and *Historic Guide to the Temple of Time.* The *Temple of Time* was a unique invention, a chart on which the world's history from "Creation to the Present Time" was set forth. The chart pictured a temple with pillars in groups of ten, each pillar representing a century and inscribed with the name of the period's outstanding sovereign. On the floor of the temple, the principal nations of the world were grouped. Important battles were listed on the right-hand margin, and on the left, the epochs from Willard's *Universal History.* The roof was emblazoned with the names of heroes.

There was considerable demand for the *Temple of Time,* and at the World's Fair in London in 1851, Mrs. Willard was awarded a gold medal for this original plan. She, herself, was extremely enthusiastic about it, feeling that it had revolutionized the teaching of history and would save time for both teacher and pupil. "We have great need," she declared, "to quicken the process of education to meet the demands of a new age of steam and electricity. We must learn to value the time of children."

She was indefatigable in giving demonstrations of teaching history with the *Temple of Time.* She personally taught every history class at the Seminary to illustrate the advantages of the new method, and spent four weeks in Philadelphia introducing it into the school conducted by her niece, Helen Phelps. This kept her very busy, but as she wrote in a letter to a friend, she preferred the name of teacher to that of lady-loafer.

As her textbooks became more popular, she found to her indignation that they were being attacked by Marcius Willson, a competitor in the field, who claimed that his books should be used in the schools, rather than hers, because hers were filled with errors. A succession of controversial pamphlets followed. Defending her reputation as a historian, Mrs. Willard published *An Appeal against Wrong and Injury, Written by Emma Willard in Answer to a Pam-*

phlet Issued by Marcius Willson and Widely Circulated Injuring Her Books and *An Appeal to Public Especially Those Concerned in Education.* She also reprinted from the *Boston Traveler* a most favorable review of her *History of the United States; or Republic of America:* "Bancroft has written us a noble history. It will live as long as the story which it so well records. But Bancroft's work is a grand and vast one, like our own Niagara, and interminable forests, and boundless prairies. . . . It was fitting too, that the intelligent young ladies of our land should have a history in which they could delight. But Mrs. Willard's work has not alone the grace of woman's pen. It has other useful qualities. In perfect arrangement, comprehensiveness, and well-digested detail, it is the best book for reference of any published."

Through the ever-increasing prestige of its founder, the Troy Female Seminary continued to prosper. In spite of the many sister institutions that had sprung up throughout the country, including Mary Lyon's endowed Seminary at Mount Holyoke, the growth of the Troy Female Seminary was such that an additional building was erected in 1846—a large building, five stories high and fifty feet square, heated by steam and lighted by gas. According to the six prominent men who acted as Examination Committee in 1845, this Seminary had "the same superiority over other Female Seminaries which Harvard and Yale have over colleges of more recent date."

16 Woman's Sphere and Woman's Rights

The country had been startled and amused in 1848 by what the newspapers called an "Insurrection among Women." The first Woman's Rights Convention, to which they referred, had been held in Seneca Falls, New York, July 19 and 20, 1848, and there a group of women had issued a Declaration of Sentiments, patterned after the Declaration of Independence, and Resolutions, outlining their aims and demands. Denied the right to take part in Antislavery and Temperance Conventions, having their sphere mapped out for them by pious clergymen claiming undue familiarity with God's will, and feeling keenly the injustice of their legal disabilities, a few courageous women had assembled to demand their rights. In spite of the indignant reaction of the press and clergy and ridicule from the public, they continued their efforts for justice. Foremost among them was one of Mrs. Willard's former pupils, Elizabeth Cady Stanton, who proposed the most controversial resolution, debated in the Convention: "Resolved, That it is the duty of the women of this country to secure to themselves their sacred right to the elective franchise."

Mrs. Willard was not a party to this Convention. The ballot seemed unimportant to her in comparison with the value of education for women, and she was convinced that education rather than agitation would solve women's problems. Yet, it is hard to imagine Emma Willard with her interest in history, current events, and politics, refusing the ballot if it were offered to her. Although she herself was continually stepping out of women's proscribed sphere and had widened that sphere for many women, she did not give her support to the efforts of Lucretia Mott and Elizabeth Cady Stanton, to implement the Convention, nor later to Susan B. Anthony. There is no doubt, however, that she sympathized to some extent with their rebellion against women's legal disabilities, from which she herself had suffered. As early as 1833, in her second address on the *Advancement of Female Education,* she pointed out some of the laws which discriminated unjustly against women: the laws which gave a husband absolute right over his wife's property, even that accumulated by her own labor; which gave him the right to will to his children her property, including the copyrights of her own books, thus making her utterly dependent on the children.

She acknowledged the injustice of these laws but said, "I leave this matter to the reflection of those who regulate the law, and to the many educated women who are rising up, and who will hereafter be capable of investigating our rights, and explaining our claims." Her work, she felt, was to educate women and through education to free them. Having been before the public for so many years as one of the leading advocates of women's education, she felt that she must keep herself above reproach, nurturing all the womanly virtues and never exposing herself to slurring attacks from the press. She did hope, however, that when women were adequately educated, all the other necessary freedoms would naturally follow.

In spite of all her difficulties with legislators in securing support and financial aid for woman's education, she seemed to have sublime faith that in God's good time, noble men would honor virtuous women by conferring upon them the rights and privileges of which they were worthy. She had made this very clear in a poem, "Prophetic Strains," published in 1830:

> Listen. The deep prophetic voice doth speak
> Of woman. There shall be a council held
> Of matrons, having powers to legislate
> In woman's province, and to recommend
> To man's prime rule, acknowledged first and best,
> As wife to husband, whatsoever, to her
> Maternal eye, seems for the general good.
>
> Such council yet shall be; but distant far the day.
> And let no woman's rash, ambitious hand,
> Attempt to urge it. Let it come, as it will,
> By God's own providence. . . .
>
> And much must woman learn, and much reflect,
> Ere she such council could with profit hold.
> And let my warning voice again be heard.

Let not the day be urg'd: wait God's full time. . . .
Let woman wait, till men shall seek her aid.
A day will come, when legislative men,
Pressed by stupendous dangers to the state,
Will see how woman's power, wealth, influence,
And mind of quick invention, might be turn'd
By right machinery to great account.
Then woman, prompt to aid distress, and proud
To be found worthy, will the means invent,
Concentrating her power, her aid to give;
Then form such council as the vision shows.

Eighteen years later, however, she apparently felt the time had come for women to prod men just a little for some of these rights and privileges. Not quite satisfied with the passiveness of her generation, yet not quite won over to the independence of the younger women, she published a very tactful letter in the *American Literary Magazine* of Albany, "A letter to Dupont de l'Eure on the Political Position of Women." The French were drafting a new Constitution, and she recommended that the women of France be invited to send delegates to Paris as a female body invested with powers to act for their sex and that the Constitutional Convention should give them "those advisory powers which in the family properly belong to the mother." These advisory powers, of course, she assured them, would find no place in men's deliberations on commerce, war, and foreign relations, but would be considered only when the rights, duties and liabilities of women were concerned.

She went so far as to say that there were certain public duties which she eventually hoped to see turned over to women—the care of the schools for young children, especially with regard to religious, moral, and intellectual training; the care of female education beyond the primary school; the care of the poor and of public morals. She made several startling assertions: that in framing of new constitutions, slaves were kindly remembered but the women forgotten; that women were persons and as such their rights were sacred; that since women had not been barred from succession to sovereignty—and Isabella, Elizabeth, Maria Theresa, and Catherine II had proved that women were not unequal to questions of law or policy, women should no longer be regarded as incapable of judging their own rights and responsibilities. Such sentiments were more characteristic of the scorned women at Seneca Falls than of Emma Willard, who for once must have forgotten caution and voiced her own real feelings.

In the matter of medical research, she certainly forgot caution and her prime object—to be the perfect example of the educated woman. In 1846, one year before any woman had been admitted as a student in a medical school in this country, Mrs. Willard published *A Treatise on the Motive Powers Which Produce the Circulation of the Blood.* It was a bold thing to do in an age when no perfect lady could make a scientific study of the human body. In fact, so bitter was the feeling about such study that when Elizabeth Blackwell, in 1847, finally gained permission to attend the Geneva Medical College, women at her boardinghouse refused to speak to her and drew away their skirts to avoid contamination when they met her on the street. Emma Willard, however, was so interested in the subject, that she gave no serious thought to critical comments. She had worked over her theory for years, had observed post-mortem examinations of the heart and lungs with her family physician, Dr. Robbins, and with Professor Smith of Troy, both believers in her theory. Now she felt it was her mission to present it to the world. In fact, she was so obsessed with the theory of Circulation by Respiration, worked so much over it during the remainder of her life, and made such courageous efforts to have it accepted by medical men that her family and friends often referred to her "unfortunate mania" on the subject. Her first treatise was followed three years later by *Respiration and Its Effects, Particularly As Respects Asiatic Cholera.*

Her theory eventually won advocates, was defended and discussed in medical journals, and finally was called "the American theory" rather than "the Willardian." Mrs. Willard had often remarked that when the theory was accepted, she would not be given credit for its discovery. "The time I spent in devotion to this theory," she wrote in the *New York Medical Journal,* "the many rebuffs I had met in seeking to promulgate it—sometimes, unhappily, affecting my social life—had made painful the duty of publishing it. My historical works had been received with favor; but I believed that in publishing this, it would be charged against me that I chose a subject unsuited to my sex."

She had the satisfaction, however, of being honored by membership in the Association for the Advancement of Science. She also
had an appeal for advice from young Dr. Elizabeth Blackwell who,
in her study of medicine, was facing one obstacle after another. Regarding Mrs. Willard as sympathetic to her search for more medical
knowledge and knowing her to be a seasoned traveler as well, Dr.
Blackwell wrote her of her plans to go to Paris and the opposition
she encountered from well-meaning friends who warned, "You, a
young, unmarried lady, go to Paris, that city of fearful immorality
. . . where insult will attend you at every step. . . ."

"Is this not a false view, a greatly exaggerated fear?" she asked
Mrs. Willard. "Is it not perfectly true everywhere that a woman
who respects herself will be respected by others; that where the life
is directed by a strong, pure motive to a noble object, in a quiet,
dignified, but determined manner, the better feelings of mankind
are enlisted, and the woman excites esteem and respectful sympathy?
. . . I trust your more experienced judgment will confirm my opinion."

It did.

In 1852, Emma Willard once more unsuccessfully petitioned
the New York Legislature for an endowment for the Troy Female
Seminary to give it permanency, and asked that they provide for the
education of their daughters as well as their sons without distinction.
Yet, in 1853, when Susan B. Anthony was trying to win for women
more active participation in the New York State Teachers' Association, and proposed Emma Willard as a candidate for vice-president,
thinking she would lend a hand in improving the opportunities and
salaries of women teachers, Mrs. Willard declined, refusing to be
drawn into Susan B. Anthony's rebellion against men's hard-and-fast
control over the Teachers' Association.

The warnings of orthodox religion in regard to women's sphere
continued to color Mrs. Willard's views. Year by year, she became
more devoted to her church, and the doctrines attributed to St. Paul
never lost their hold on her. Yet, ultramodern theories occasionally
crowded out the orthodox. She advocated the financial independence
of women, urging them to give up the idea that they must be supported in order to be respectable, or that they must marry in order to

be supported. In her *Morals for the Young, or Good Principles In-stilling Wisdom,* published in 1857, she wrote: "In making her calculations for the future, . . . every young woman is wise to prepare herself to become independent, useful, and happy, without marriage; although her education should always fit her for those high and holy duties, which result from marriage and maternity."

She had seen a great change in public opinion toward the education of women in the preceding thirty years. Consternation at women's study of geometry, history, the sciences, and even physiology was disappearing. Nevertheless anything new still aroused opposition, as for example the examinations in philosophy at the Troy Female Seminary, which critics said were a fraud perpe-trated upon the public because women could not possibly compre-hend the meaning of philosophical statements and could only memorize them as they did Greek of Sanskrit. These accusations were answered by the Examining Committee of prominent men who assured the public that there was no conspiracy between teachers and pupils, that in a searching examination they had found the young ladies intelligent students of philosophy. Another innovation at the Seminary was the appointment of a woman, Mary A. Hastings, as the head of the Science Department. She was one of the first women to give laboratory lectures with experiments, and her courses on mechanics and chemistry were said to equal those at Yale. Mrs. Willard herself, again pioneered when she published in 1853, a textbook on astronomy, *Astronography, or Astronomical Geography.* Of it Professor Avery of Hamilton College said: "She has achieved a remarkable success in making the elements of a difficult science, easy of comprehension."

She continued to add to her list of American history textbooks, publishing in 1849 *Last Leaves of American History,* which recorded the Mexican War and the history of California. This was followed in 1856 by a revised edition which she called *Late American History: Containing a Full Account of the Courage, Conduct and Success of John C. Frémont; by Which through Many Hardships and Sufferings, He Became the Hero of California.* As Frémont was then being considered as a presidential candidate, this book was advertised as giving an "impartial, copious account of his career."

Mrs. Willard had become very much interested in the exploration of the Far West, in the Mormons, in the gold rush of '49, and in the ever-increasing number of immigrants who were flooding the country. She was alarmed by the steady influx of foreigners attracted by Northern industry, and felt that these immigrants, unused to our customs and standards, were largely responsible for the too frequent riots, robberies, and assassinations in New York, Philadelphia, and Baltimore.

She was troubled, too, about the Mormons, and wrote Senator Thomas A. Benton of Missouri: "I feel uneasy about the Mormons getting possession of such a central and important part of the country. There is, it seems to me, a spirit of false liberality out, which fails to see the real danger that may accrue from allowing that people to organize a State with their peculiar institutions; and I feel the more on this subject as the progress of the sect involves, as I have reason to believe, the degradation of my own sex; and, if of my sex, certainly the deterioration of the whole of society." Then she added: "We were born a *Protestant Christian* nation. . . . If we tolerate others that is enough. We should not allow them to form governments or exercise political powers on any other basis. . . . If they want to do this, let them go elsewhere. . . ."

She was heartily in favor of building a railroad to the Far West and wrote Senator Benton: "Your views concerning the great central railroad I regard not only as just, but of the utmost importance, but for this connecting link, which now, in imagination, holds them to their native land, I think there is great reason to apprehend that California and Oregon would soon unite and form a separate nation, which would be unfortunate for us all. . . ."

While writing *Late American History,* she carried on a lively correspondence not only with Senator Benton, but with other prominent men in Washington who could give her first-hand information, and often arranged interviews with them. She was in the gallery of the Senate in 1850 when Henry Clay delivered his famous compromise speech, which temporarily settled the bitter debate over the extension of slavery in the Western territories. So intense had been the feeling in the South, that there had been threats of secession, and in view of this, Mrs. Willard called Clay's speech "the crowning action of his useful life." She made a summary of the speech for her history and sent it to him to learn if he were satisfied with it. His reply was: "Perfectly."

Meanwhile, her friend, Sarah Josepha Hale, had edited *Woman's Record: or Sketches of all Distinguished Women from the Beginning to A.D. 1850, arranged in Four Eras with Selections from Female Writers of Every Age.* This book, published by Harper and Brothers, ranked Mrs. Willard among the distinguished women of the world and she was very happy over the tribute. A sketch of her life and work, her picture, her *Ocean Hymn, Rocked in the Cradle of the Deep,* and three selections of her prose works gave her an imposing share of space.

In the summer of 1854, she made up her mind to attend the World's Educational Convention in London, not only because she was vitally interested in the cause of education, but because she felt women educators should be represented there. As her son John was not free to travel with her because of his duties at the Seminary, Jane Lincoln was her companion. In London, she was warmly welcomed by Henry Barnard who introduced her to prominent educators of every country. After several months of travel on the Continent, she returned to Troy, well satisfied with her expedition but troubled at the dissension in her own country over the extension of slavery.

17   Saving the Union

Probably no other woman in America was as familiar with her country's history as Mrs. Willard, or better informed on current events. As she observed the increasing antislavery agitation and the bitterness between the North and the South, she grew more and more apprehensive. Her ears rang with the prophecies of foreign statesmen that America was doomed to destruction, and she resolved to do everything in her power to preserve the Union.

Although she believed slavery to be fundamentally wrong, she was not an abolitionist. As the friend of many Southerners, she felt she understood their point of view and could do much to bring the North and the South together. She identified herself with the American Colonization Society whose object was to solve the slavery problem by establishing a Negro republic in Africa and by aiding the emigration of free Negroes. In this she again separated herself from Lucretia Mott, Elizabeth Cady Stanton, and Susan B. Anthony, who worked actively with the abolitionists.

With concern, Emma Willard saw her fellow Americans deeply stirred by the publication of *Uncle Tom's Cabin*. She read with anxiety reports of the debates on the Kansas-Nebraska Bill, of the civil war in Kansas, and of the speeches of Sumner, Seward, and Chase, attacking slavery and accusing the South of a breach of faith. Brooks' assault upon Sumner, the Dred Scott Decision, and John Brown's raid followed, one close upon the other. She watched the rise of that impelling man from the West, Abraham Lincoln. She recognized his justice and potential greatness, and like the rest of her countrymen, she eagerly followed his debates with Douglas. She stood aghast at Seward's prophecy of "irrepressible conflict," and read in dismay Lincoln's dynamic words: "A house divided against itself can not stand."

She felt as if a vast tidal wave were engulfing the nation and that she must stop it. She wrote many letters to prominent statesmen, pleading for peace and for the preservation of the Union. She was sure that the breach could be healed by more wisdom, by more efforts at conciliation. In the presidential campaign of 1860, her sympathies naturally were with the Constitutional Unionists, headed by John Bell and Edward Everett, for like the men of this party who shrank from conflict, she felt that high-sounding phrases and good resolutions would still save the Union. She was not alarmed by the election of Lincoln, for she had confidence in him and the Republican party, but when several Southern States threatened secession, she sent many appeals to the newspapers, in an effort to avert this.

Her *Appeal to South Carolina*, published in the New York *Express*, December 19, 1860, was a desperate cry for peace at any price, and in it, she strayed far from her old-time clarity of reasoning, making some pitifully weak concessions to slavery. She called attention to the fact that the condition of the Negro in Africa was far below that of American servitude, stressing *servitude* not *slavery*, for as she expressed it, "The master owns not the man, but his time. He has a perpetual servant, not a slave." As the Negroes were here, she reasoned, and incapable of taking care of themselves, Southerners would be obliged to care for them, and must then necessarily have the benefit of their labor. She urged South Carolina not to secede, warning that peaceful secession was impossible as the Union must be preserved.

After South Carolina seceded, Mrs. Willard presented to Congress a *Memorial from American Women*, which received approval from the few, but which William H. Seward criticized as advocating slavery. Nevertheless, she persevered, indomitable as ever at seventy-four. In February, 1861, she went to Washington, hoping she could influence some of the political leaders then holding a peace convention.

"I felt I must come," she wrote her daughter-in-law, "and I feel that the voice of the women in this crisis will not be unheeded, but will tend to peace. . . . My sister [Almira] and her sweet daughter are here with me; and my sister has exerted herself to get signatures to my memorial. I have modified it since it was first sent out, as the ultras on both sides objected to it, while some (judicious people, as I think) believe it will do much good by calling attention from mere political considerations to those of right and duty. This change . . .

and other causes made such a delay in the affair of getting signatures at New York that I shall not have as many as I expected from there. But Troy has done and is doing very well, and Philadelphia has already sent me a goodly number and I am to receive more. The memorial is now circulating in Washington, Baltimore, and other places. . . . In undertaking to do something, though a little, for our beloved country, in this her hour of peril, I find I am but doing what many expected of me."

The Memorial with its four thousand signatures was presented to the Senate by Senator Crittenden of Kentucky and to the House of Representatives by John A. Gilmer of North Carolina. "Our humble petition," it began, "is that those to whom in our feebleness, we look for help, will not allow party or sectional prejudices to prevail over a spirit of mutual conciliation. . . ." With it was a statement signed by nine men from the various political parties, assuring Congress that they saw nothing unbecoming in such a memorial from American women.

Many friendly, pathetic letters passed between Mr. and Mrs. Gilmer and Mrs. Willard during the trying months, that followed and continued for a time after the fall of Fort Sumter, showing how overwhelmed they all were by the course of events. "If I thought that the Northern armies were going to make aggressive war on the South," wrote Mrs. Willard to Mrs. Gilmer, "I should feel as unhappy about it as you would. So would the greater part of the Northern people. . . . Who knows but the women may yet contrive some way of peace, for we love one another South and North, and Christian women will watch for opportunities to make peace, and pray that peace and righteousness may prevail."

Mrs. Willard, however, heartily endorsed the North's determination to put down the rebellion. To her sister, Mrs. Phelps, who was in Baltimore when it was occupied by Northern troops, she wrote that in her opinion the North should firmly hold the sword in one hand and proffer the olive branch with the other. "Let them show plainly that they have no thought to *conquer* the South by force of arms," she added, "but that their *ultimatum* is this—the Government shall not be illegally broken up."

She could not refrain from writing President Lincoln whom she felt needed support and encouragement during these critical days. "Presuming that I am known to you as a writer of my country's history," she said, "and having just heard that the great cares which weigh upon you begin to tell upon your physical health, I determined to write to you my high approval of your general course and leading measures."

Mrs. Willard was soon busy with plans to aid the families of volunteers, and was made president of the Associate Relief Society of Troy women, organized at the Seminary to furnish hospital supplies and clothing for the soldiers.

Mrs. Elizabeth F. Ellet, the author of *Women of the Revolution* and *Pioneer Women of the West,* came to Troy to talk with her and to bring a message from the ladies of New York City, asking what they could do for peace. Peace was still foremost in Mrs. Willard's mind, and even while she was busy with her work for the soldiers, she was evolving a plan.

In May, 1862, with the publication of *Via Media,* she offered her solution for the problem of Negro Slavery, which had so far baffled all the statesmen of the country. The subtitle of *Via Media* read: *The African in America: To Find His True Position and Place Him in It, the Via Media on Which the North and the South Might Meet in a Permanent and Happy Settlement.* She stated definitely that political equality for the Negro would be a menace to the country and that only educated white men should be given political power. Assuming that God had intended to rank the Negroes as servants and had, by their color, marked them for this province, she suggested "regulated servitude." As God had sanctioned the servants' place in the family by the Ten Commandments, she believed He might possibly have had it in mind to create a race to serve white women and add strength to their physical weakness. Liberia, she admitted, had not proved to be the solution of the slavery problem, for neither free Negroes nor slaves were willing to migrate, and four million Negroes in this country had to be dealt with intelligently and justly. In her opinion, they needed the supervision of a master and in return the master was entitled to their services.

She recommended that the slave market be abolished and that families should not be cruelly separated. She suggested that talented Negroes be freed and sent to Liberia where the best Negroes were needed. All this could be accomplished, she felt, through a tribunal of the best American statesmen. She suggested that the President and Congress appoint commissioners to deal with the large number of slaves which the war had put in the Government's hands and recommended that Northern families take one or two of them into their homes. Then, after ten or fifteen years of service, when they would be "fitted" to go to Liberia, their employers would be bound to send them. Or, if they did not wish to go to Liberia and preferred to stay in service during their lifetime, laws should be made to regulate this servitude. Such a solution of the Negro problem, she maintained, would also solve the servant problem for the Northern housewife and in many cases would avert death and invalidism for the conscientious overworked woman.

In spite of all her hopes for the conciliating powers of *Via Media,* it received little attention in the onrush of events. A few praised it, among them General McClennan, who assured her that the views set forth were identical with his own, and that had the power been placed in his hands, he would have tried to establish such a system as she advocated. Her nephew, John Willard, however, now Judge of the Supreme Court of New York, frankly wrote her that the time for the adoption of such a plan was long past and that to press it on the country at this moment would do more harm than good.

Emma Willard's next effort for the Union was her National Hymn, "Our Country," sold for the benefit of the United States Sanitary Commission, the relief organization sponsored by the Government. In it, she gave full expression of her patriotic sentiments:

> God save America!
> God grant our standard may
>   Where e'er it wave;
> Follow the just and right,
> Foremost be in the fight,
> And glorious still in might
>   Our own to save.

> CHORUS— Father Almighty!
>   Humbly, we crave,
>   Save thou America,
>   Our Country save.

God keep America!
Of Nations great and free
    Man's noblest friend:
Still with the ocean bound
Our continent around,
Each State in place be found,
    Till time shall end.

God bless America!
As in our Father's day,
    So evermore.
God grant all discords cease,
Kind brotherhoods increase,
And truth and love breathe peace
    From shore to shore!

"God save America" was Mrs. Willard's continued prayer throughout the war.

18   Looking Forward

Mrs. Willard rejoiced over the progress of General Grant's troops in the West, grateful that the Union was being upheld; yet she grieved over the plight of her Southern friends, and resolved to dedicate the rest of her life to peace. Conferring with Elihu Burritt, whose League of Universal Brotherhood held an annual Peace Conference in Europe, she began to plan a trip to Europe in 1863, to work for peace. She gave this up because of the objections of her family, and instead drew up another peace plan similar to the one she had published in 1820. This plan, published in 1864, she called simply *Universal Peace*. Once more she suggested that the nations of the world form a permanent judicial tribunal to which by mutual consent, their disputes be referred, and again she chose Jerusalem as the seat of this tribunal. Such an organization, she explained, was much more possible now than in 1820 because of the wonderful inventions—ocean steamers and the telegraph. Delegates to the Permanent Peace Council could reside in Jerusalem for a term of years and might easily be accompanied by their families. She had chosen Jerusalem because of Bible prophecies and because the choice of any other city would arouse national jealousies. Although the Holy Land was under the control of the Turks, she thought England and France, who had influence with Turkey, might arrange to buy it. The Rothschilds, she felt sure, would gladly furnish the money for the cause of universal peace and could build a railroad to the coast and do whatever was necessary to prepare for a meeting of the Council. France, England, Russia, and America should inaugurate this Council and when delegates from all the nations assembled, they should prepare a code of international laws which would bind all nations. The Gentiles of the world should then aid the Jews to return to Jerusalem and thus fulfill Bible prophecy. Had this Council been in existence before the Civil War, she maintained, the South could have laid her complaints before it and bloodshed might have been averted. Emma Willard, in 1864, was looking far ahead to the

League of Nations, to the World Court, to the United Nations, and to the State of Israel.

Next, she brought her *American History* up to date. Her publisher had many calls for history textbooks, especially from the South, and as most of those available offended Southern educators, her books were in demand. With growing concern, she watched the progress of Reconstruction, drawing her own conclusions, which she confided to her nephew, General John Wolcott Phelps, whose military career she had followed with great interest. She was proud of his Civil War record in the lower Mississippi Valley and respected his independent opinions, even if she did not always agree with them. Now she wrote him: "When Andrew Johnson first began his administration, I had hopes he would improve matters. . . . and I wrote a letter to Mr. J——— suggesting to him the satisfaction it might give, if he would build up Negrodom by sending to Liberia an Ambassador and Minister Plenipotentiary, who should also be an American agent for that country and we obtain the right to send members to a congress there, our Negroes choosing those who would then be persuaded to go. Now if Mr. J——— would have heard this —I had other plans ahead. You, whom I think the Lord has made for some extra-ordinary thing—I designed should have been this Envoy and Agent—and the likeliest Negro in America, Fred Douglass, The Secretary of the Legation. Now see how well my plans tally with yours, as expressed in your letter to me—If the Lord had seen fit in his Providence, to have us two to arrange the affairs of the nation just at this particular time—that would have been done which now there is no hope of. But as changes for the worse have been, we can but hope that hereafter there may be changes for the better. . . ."

Even though her plans for the country were not bearing fruit, she was receiving considerable attention in magazines and currently published books. In the *American Journal of Education,* there was a long, appreciative article, *Educational Services of Mrs. Emma Willard* by Henry Fowler of the University of Rochester, and this later was included in *Memories of Teachers, Educators, and Promoters and Benefactors of Education, Literature, and Science.* Mrs. Willard was the only woman represented in this volume with Ezekiel Cheever, Caleb Bingham, William C. Woodbridge, Horace Mann, and Timothy Dwight of Yale. She furnished Professor Fowler with a great deal of the material for his article and spent many happy hours reliving her struggles and conquests. She also sent data about her life and work in Middlebury to Samuel Swift for his *History of the Town of Middlebury*.

When G. H. Hollister's *History of Connecticut* was published, she was proud to find the comment: "Mrs. Sigourney, Mrs. Ann S. Stephens, and Mrs. Emma Willard are among the most gifted and eminent writers of our country." Mrs. Elizabeth Ellet, who in her books was giving women a place in the historical records of their country, mentioned both Mrs. Willard and Mrs. Phelps in *The Queens of American Society*. In *Eminent Women of the Age, Being Narratives of the Lives and Deeds of the Most Prominent Women of the Present Generation*, a compilation of biographical sketches by James Parton, Horace Greeley, Thomas Wentworth Higginson, Elizabeth Cady Stanton, and others, Mrs. Willard was given an important place under the section, "Our Pioneer Educators." In 1869, she was elected an honorary member of Sorosis, the first woman's club in the United States, which that year had been founded in New York. In accepting, she said: "I shall expect a great deal of this society of gifted women, and I hope that in laying out your plans you will not make your boundaries so fixed that you cannot enlarge them and have room to grow. It has been my experience that in beginning anything new, we cannot see at the outset all that is to come of it, and it is well to be careful not to plant our oak in a flower pot."

Emma Willard continued to live in the small red-brick house on the Seminary grounds and for some years her congenial companion and secretary was Mrs. Celia Burr. They lived happily together in spite of Mrs. Burr's decided leanings toward woman's rights and other liberal movements of the day. In fact, Mrs. Burr's influence helped counteract in great measure the determined reactionary influence of Mrs. Phelps, who in the early 1870's became active in the Anti-Woman Suffrage Society, headed by Mrs. Madeleine Dahlgren and Mrs. W. T. Sherman. A Sixteenth Amendment providing for woman suffrage, was before Congress at this time, sponsored by the National Woman Suffrage Association. This Mrs. Phelps and her associates opposed, Mrs. Phelps often giving the impression that her sister, Mrs. Willard, shared her sentiments. This impression Mrs. Burr did her best to dispel. She had left Mrs. Willard in 1865 to marry William H. Burleigh, well known in antislavery circles, but corresponded frequently with her.

In April, 1871, an article, *Mrs. Emma Willard and the Woman Question,* by Mrs. Burleigh, appeared in the *Woman's Journal,* a woman suffrage paper, published in Boston and edited by Lucy Stone. "It is with no little surprise," wrote Mrs. Burleigh, "that I have lately seen the name of Mrs. Emma Willard associated with an anti-woman's rights movement—a name that fifty years ago was the synonym of a radicalism so pronounced, so much in advance of the public sentiment of the time, that the suffrage movement of today is tame in comparison with it. During the whole of her long and useful life, Mrs. Willard was an extremist on the subject of woman's rights and duties. . . . She insisted that government could never be rightly administered till woman had a voice in making the laws. . . . She was not a believer in universal but in educated suffrage, but if she ever held sex to be a necessary disqualification for suffrage, it must have been years ago, before the writer made her acquaintance."

To prove her statements, Mrs. Burleigh quoted from letters written to her by Mrs. Willard in 1868 and 1869. "Thank you for the newspaper scraps about your new society in which I feel a deep interest," Mrs. Willard had said. "Feeling, as I do, that women are still far from having that influence for good which they ought to have, I am glad of this effort on the part of cultivated women to get together and see what they can do to make the world better."

A year later, Mrs. Willard wrote her: "Since my visit to you I have thought a good deal of our talks about women's voting. You will remember what I have said so often, that we have too much voting already, and I think so; but if having the ballot will give women the power which they need, and enable them to put a stop to these terrible wars, I am in favor of their having it. The State can no more do without woman's tenderness and motherly wisdom than can the family. That I have been preaching all my life, and if there is any way in which people can be made to see it, I shall be glad."

Later, hearing from Mrs. Burleigh that she had become a public lecturer, she wrote her: "My first feeling . . . was one of regret; but now that I know your reasons for doing so, and that you have your husband's approval, I cannot withhold mine. After all, you have only entered now upon a work that I took up more than half a century ago—pleading the cause of my sex. I did it in my way, you are doing it in yours, and as I have reason to believe that God blessed me in my efforts, I pray that he will bless you in yours. I wish I might hear you speak. . . . I see frequent references to you in the papers, and I read with interest all that relates to you and your work. I am more and more convinced that it is a good work and one that will lead to good. As for me, my days of toil are over, and I must soon go to my rest; but I am glad to think that what I began alone and in the face of much opposition will be carried forward by able workers, and lead to great results; that the State will by-and-by, like the family, be controlled by the united wisdom of men and women."

After Celia Burr's marriage, Sarah Willard, a granddaughter, took charge of Mrs. Willard's household, and another young relative, a nephew, William Hart, made his home with them. William had come to prepare for Yale, as Aunt Willard insisted she could teach him as well as anyone, but instead of going to Yale, William helped John Hart Willard with the management of the Seminary, and later went into business in Troy. He lived with Aunt Willard for many years, even after his marriage, and two of his children were born in her home. His little daughter, Helen, and Mrs. Willard were great friends. Helen always thought of Aunt Willard in a black silk dress with a full skirt, a tight-fitting basque, a fluffy tulle fichu, and in a white cap which set off her gray curls.

No reception or dancing class at the Seminary was complete without Mrs. Willard. Enthroned in a big armchair, she sat at the foot of the stairs, and the girls coming down two by two curtsied as they passed her. They respected her, were in awe of her, and loved her. She still attended the annual examination. As the years went by, she grew more affectionate, gentle, and tolerant, while remaining as cheerful, companionable, and witty as she had been at forty. Her interest in public affairs continued, and she enjoyed discussing them. There was always a new book on her table, and beside it the latest newspapers and magazines. Nothing gave her more pleasure than to gather her family about her on Sunday evenings and hear them repeat passages from the Bible which to her was still the Book of books. She had studied Greek and Hebrew after she was fifty, in order to read it in the original.

When finally, at eighty-three, she moved to the Seminary building where she could be nearer her son and his family, she occupied a study and bedroom on the first floor. She spent hours in the study in a big chair in front of a table desk. Here, in the heart of the thriving institution which she had founded, she wrote, planned, and thought over the past, conscious always of the orderly activities of her Seminary, hearing the light footsteps of her beloved girls as they hurried to their classes. She still found great satisfaction in keeping a diary, recording her estimate of Sunday sermons and every book she read. The last entry was dated "April sixth, 1870."

On April 15, 1870, the newspapers reported her death. If at times she had failed to receive full appreciation for her labors, it was not lacking now. Praise poured in from all parts of the world. Newspapers and magazines told of her work and of the great contribution she had made toward the education of women. The Legislature of New York, which had so persistently refused to endorse or carry out her recommendations for state-endowed seminaries for the higher education of women, now unanimously passed a resolution expressing appreciation of her life and work.

During those last years, as Mrs. Willard had sat in her big armchair reflecting on the past and future progress of women, she had seen with satisfaction and a glow of happiness the unprecedented steps which were being taken in woman's education. Vassar Female College had been founded nearby in Poughkeepsie, New York, in 1861, by Matthew Vassar, who said: "It occurred to me that woman, having received from her Creator the same intellectual constitution as man, has the same right as man to intellectual culture and development." Four years later, Vassar Female College, the first fully-endowed institution in the world for the higher education of women, had opened its doors, and in accordance with the wishes of the founder, women had taken their places with men on the faculty. It seems incredible that such events could have transpired without letters of comment or encouragement from Mrs. Willard, but none have been found, and as most of Matthew Vassar's correspondence was sold by a nephew to a ragman, it is highly probable that Emma Willard's comments on Vassar College were lost in this way.

Wesleyan Female College, Elmira College, Mary Sharp College, and other colleges for women had also been established in the West and South; there was Antioch College in Ohio, under the guidance of Horace Mann; and in the Far West, Iowa State University and the University of Utah had been opened as co-educational institutions. These all became possible because the Troy Female Seminary had proved that women were capable of comprehending higher studies and were unharmed by them.

Many other signs of the advancement of women had brightened Mrs. Willard's last days. The war had made it necessary for women to take the place of men in teaching, in business, in industry, and on the farms. Even in the field hospitals women had made a place for themselves and brought order, cleanliness, and comfort through the efforts of Dr. Elizabeth Blackwell and Dorothea Dix who provided trained nurses, of Clara Barton and many others who served as nurses, and of Dr. Mary Walker, the one woman serving as physician at the front. Anna Ella Carroll had saved Maryland for the Union and had been a trusted advisor of President Lincoln. In the settlement of the West, women were courageously making a valuable contribution, bringing education, religion, and order to the frontier.

Mrs. Willard had begun to see the fulfillment of her prophecy, made in 1818, that educated women would have much to give their country. She glimpsed only faintly what the future would bring, but she knew that women had seen the vision and would go forward.

Index

Adams, John, 4, 29, 49
Adams, John Quincy, 49
Adams, Hannah, 65
Advancement of Female Education, 88, 116
Albany *Evening Journal,* 65
American Colonization Society, 123
American History, 130
American Journal of Education, 130
American Ladies' Magazine, 63, 89, 98
American Literary Magazine, 117
American Quarterly Review, 89, 90
Amherst College, 55
Ancient Geography, 40
Anthony, Susan B., 115, 119, 123
Antioch College, 135
Anti-Woman Suffrage Society, 131
Appeal Against Wrong and Injury, 113, 114
Appeal to the Public, 114
Appeal to South Carolina, 124
Association for the Advancement of Science, 119
Astronomical Geography, 120
Avery, Professor, 120

Bancroft, George, 114
Barnard, Henry, 103, 107, 112, 122
Barnes, A. S., 108
Barton, Clara, 135
Beecher, Catherine, 61, 62, 87, 100
Bell, John, 124
Belloc, Madame Louise, 78, 79, 96
Benton, Thomas A., 121
Bingham, Caleb, 130
Blackwell, Dr. Elizabeth, 118, 119, 135

Boston High School for Girls, 61
Boston *Traveler,* 65, 114
Botsford, Mrs., 9
Brandegee, Lucy, 3
Brooks, Preston, 123
Brown, John, 123
Burleigh, William H., 132
Burleigh, Mrs. William H., 131-133
Burr, Celia, *see* Burleigh, Mrs. William H.
Burritt, Elihu, 104, 127
Burritt, Elizah, 58

Calhoun, John, 20
Campbell, Duncan, 29
Carroll, Anna Ella, 135
Cass, Governor, 46, 53
Catherine II, 117
Charles X, 73, 75
Chase, Salmon P., 123
Cheever, Ezekiel, 130
Cheever, George Barrell, 87
Choiseul, Count de, 85
Cincinnati *Gazette,* 65
Civil War, 124, 130
Clay, Henry, 20, 121, 122
Clinton, DeWitt, 28, 37, 54, 56, 57
Combe, George, 29, 99
Connecticut Common School Journal, 106, 107
Cooper, James Fenimore, 72, 79
Corday, Charlotte, 73
Crittenden, Senator, 125
Cuvier, Baron, 78

Dahlgren, Madeleine, 131
Davidson, Lucretia, 94
Dix, Dorothea, 135

136